MAKING INTERIOR MODELS
インテリア模型製作

Susumu Kurabayashi
倉林　進

インテリア
模型製作
MAKING
INTERIOR MODELS

知っていると役立つ方法

製作編

CONTENTS

　インテリアデザインを学んでいる学生、新人デザイナー、コーディネーターの皆さんから紙模型では表現できない家具などの作り方の技法書はないものか、といった要望を以前から聞いていた。1987年に「室内」にて一年間模型の作り方を連載した時に多くの質問や「材料の購入場所はどこで？」などの反響が大きく、この本を作るきっかけとなった。以来、4年にわたり日常業務とのせめぎ合いに泣かされながらもようやく本書の出版にこぎ着けた。

　本書に掲載されている内容は、どちらかと言えば難しく見られがちだが、作り方や材料の選択は最適であると思う。特に道具に関しては、プロが使う道具や機械は使わず一般的な道具だけで作っている。

　例えば、中に掲載されている白木の椅子の作り方にしても、従来ならばバルサや角材を使い、木工ボンドで苦労して組み立てていた。しかしここでは、なじみのないABS板という材料で作っているが、切ったり曲げたりするのが容易で、最適な材料だと確信している。

　私が教えているモデリングコースの学生に実験的に本書中の題材を作らせてみたところ、かなり良い答えが返ってきた。

　モデリングとしては、デザイナーが自分のイメージ、アイデアの確認や展開のために作るエスキースモデルや第三者にデザインの意図を伝達し理解を求めるために作るフィニッシュモデルがある。本書で製作しているものは後者であり、その形態、素材、色彩をよりリアルに作るために参考にしてもらえれば幸いである。

　これを機に、モデル作りのアドバイスや材料の供給まで幅広くモデリングに関して携わってゆきたいと考えている。

For quite some time I have gotten requests from students of interior design and new designers and coordinators for a technique manual for making models of furniture and other interior items that cannot be represented adequately with paper models. Since 1987, the year that my model-making processes were serialized in "Shitsunai" (Interiors) magazine, I have received such a big reaction and so many questions, including questions on where to buy materials, that I decided to produce this book. I worked on it for the next four years, squeezing out whatever time I could from regular workday obligations. Finally it is time now for publication.

The content of this book, one might say, consists of items that may look difficult, but whose construction process and material selection are ideal. Particularly the furniture models shown here can be made without using any professional tools or equipment--just ordinary tools.

For example, the process of making a plain wooden chair once required the use of balsa or square pieces and a painstaking assembly process using wood bond. In this book, I use the rather unfamiliar ABS board, but since this material cuts and bends easily, I consider it ideal.

I had the students in my modeling course use the techniques in this book in actual practice, and the results were quite good. In modeling, a designer uses a sketch model to confirm or develop his/her image or ideas, and a finish model to communicate to a third party one's design intentions and to gain their understanding. This book covers the latter and may be used as a reference work to aid in creating forms, materials and color that are more true to the original.

With this in mind, I have aimed to offer useful advice on model-making, including the supply of materials, to cover a wide range of areas in modeling.

装丁・レイアウト＝大貫伸樹＋伊藤庸一＋竹田恵子
Book Design = Shinju Onuki +Yoichi Ito + Keiko Takeda

撮影＝鈴木克彦
Photograph = Katsuhiko Suzuki

英訳＝(株)バベル・インターナショナル
English Translation = Babel International Inc.

協力＝勝又 都恭琴
　　　山中 保
　　　杉山正彦
　　　咸 守日
Cooperation = Miyako Katsumata
　　　　　　　Tamotsu Yamanaka
　　　　　　　Masahiko Sugiyama
　　　　　　　Ham Sooyl

MAKING INTERIOR MODELS

ISBN4-7661-0798-5

Printed in Singapore

知っていると
役立つ方法
Useful Techniques
to Know

平ヤスリを作る <small>ヤスリを作る</small>
Making a Flat File <small>*Making a file*</small>

1. ハレパネに紙ヤスリ(耐水ペーパー)を貼る。

1: Paste sandpaper (waterproof paper) onto adhesive styrene paper.

2. 使いやすい大きさに裏からカットする。表からだと刃がたたないため。

2: Cut to a usable size. Cut from the back. The blade will not grab if you cut from the front.

3. このような面をヤスリがけする場合、ヤスリの角は直角にして、削る面の幅より少し小さめに先細りさせるときれいにできる。

3: When filing this type of surface, make the edge of the file perpendicular and the end slightly narrower than the surface to be filed. This will allow you to file cleanly to the corners.

4. 鋭角部分をヤスリがけする場合、ヤスリの角を角度に合わせカットする。

4: File the sharp corner part. Cut according to the angle of the file corner.

5. このように、ヤスリの角がコーナーに入り使いやすい。

5: In this way, the angle of the file will be able to reach into the corner.

2

大きな曲面を削る ヤスリを作る
Filing a Large Curved Surface Making a file

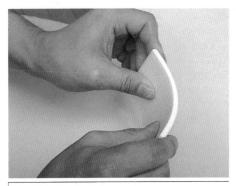

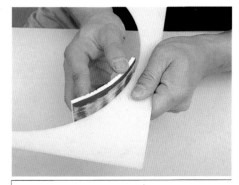

1．ハレパネの裏を3mm間隔にカッターで切れ目を入れ曲げる。

1: Put cut lines in adhesive styrene paper at 3-mm intervals with a cutter and bend.

2．このように、Rにフィットして使える。

2: In this way the file will fit a curve.

3

角材や丸材を使ったヤスリ
Files Using Squared and Round Materials

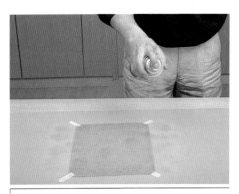

1．紙ヤスリの裏にスプレーのり（77）を吹き付ける。

1: Use spray glue (77) on the back of sandpaper.

2．ABS板やアクリル材などの角材をのせ、カッターで切り出す。

2: Place on square material such as ABS board or acrylic board and cut out with a cutter.

3．角材に貼ったヤスリ。右は2面にヤスリを貼ったもの。

3: Files made with square material, and on the right pasted onto two surfaces.

4．丸棒や丸パイプに貼ったヤスリ。

4: Files on round rods and round pipes.

4

瞬間接着剤をスポイトに入れる スポイトを使った接着法
Drawing Instant Bond into an Eye Dropper *Attaching using an eye dropper*

１．瞬間接着剤を少量スポイトに入れる。

1: Draw a bit of instant bond into the eye dropper.

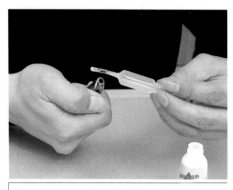

２．ライターで先を回しながらあぶり、やわらかくする。あぶりすぎて燃やさないように。

2: Heat the tip with a lighter as you turn it, so that it softens. Be careful not to overheat it or it will catch fire.

３．ピンセットで先をつまんで伸ばす。太さは、伸ばす長さで調整する。

3: Pinch and extend the tip using tweezers. Adjust the thickness and length.

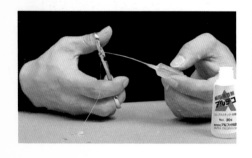

４．先を切る。点付けや、隙間への流し込みなどに便利。

4: Cut the tip. This becomes handy for squeezing bond in droplets and into narrow spaces.

5

スチのりをアルコールで溶かして使う
Diluting Styrene Glue with Alcohol for Use

１．スチのりを燃料用アルコールでよく溶き（３：１）あらかじめ先を伸ばしておいたスポイトで吸い取り、中に入れる。瞬間接着剤の時よりは口を太めにする。

1: Dilute styrene glue well with fuel grade alcohol (3:1) and draw into eye dropper. Use an eye dropper prepared with the extended tip and draw in. Make the dropper opening larger than for instant bond.

2: After it is drawn in, it can now be used for squeezing out glue in droplets or into narrow gaps.

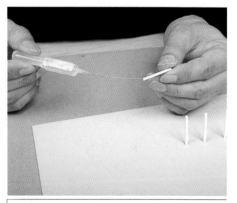

２．スポイトに入れると点付けや、隙間への流し込みに便利である。糸をひかず、またかわきも遅くなるので作業しやすい。

6

先を曲げ、上向きの接着法 スポイトを使った接着法
Bending the Tip for Upward Attachment *Attaching using an eye dropper*

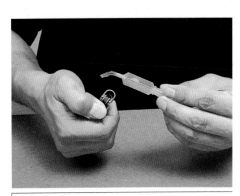

1．接着剤を入れ、ライターで先をあぶる。

1: Draw in the bonding agent and pass the tip over the flame of a lighter.

2．ピンセットでつまみ伸ばす。

2: Pinch and extend with tweezers.

3．すばやく指か丸棒にあてがい、曲げる。

3: Quickly use your finger or a round rod to bend.

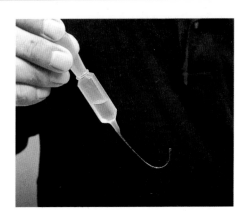

4．先を切る。空気が入らずに続けて接着剤が出せ、このように上部への接着に適する。

4: Cut the tip. In this way you can squeeze droplets of bonding agent upwards without air getting in.

7

木工ボンドに中性洗剤を入れて流し込みやすくする
Adding Neutral Detergent to Wood Bond to Make it Spread More Easily

1．容器に木工ボンドを入れ、水でよく溶き中性洗剤を1、2滴入れる。(ボンド3：水1〜2)

1: Put wood bond into a container, dilute well with water and add one or two drops of neutral detergent. (3 parts bond to 1-2 parts water)

2: Apply with a brush or draw into an eye dropper as shown here. When you squeeze on drops, it will quickly and easily spread. When you wish to apply bond to parts only, do not add neutral detergent.

2．筆で塗るか、このようにスポイトに入れ、点付けするとサッと流れ込みボンドが広がる。部分的にボンドを付けたい時は、中性洗剤を入れないように。

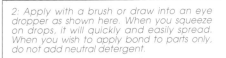

8 木工パテでスチロール系のキズや穴を埋める 木工パテの使い方
Filling in Marks or Holes in Styrol with Wood Putty *Using wood putty*

１．このような大きなキズ穴を埋めるには、スチロール系が溶けない水性系の木工パテを使うとよい。家庭用パテ、メーコー（株）製使用。

1: To fill a deep scratch like this, use water-based wood putty so that the styrol does not melt. "Putty for Household Use" by Meiko was used here.

２．木工パテをよく練り、へらで押しつけるように穴を埋める。

2: Knead the putty well, and use a spatula to press into the holes.

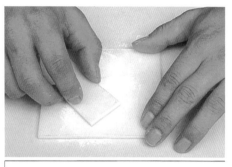

３．十分乾いたら紙ヤスリで削る。

3: Let it dry thoroughly, then sand with sandpaper.

４．出来上がり。

4: Finished.

9 パテを厚く盛るには 木工パテの使い方
To Stack Wood Putty Thickly *Using wood putty*

１．木工パテを厚く盛り、乾くと左のように割れてしまう。そこで木工パテ３に水２〜３を入れよく溶き、そこに石膏３を入れよく混ぜると木工パテだけより速く固まり、石膏だけよりは作業時間が長くとれる。乾いても右のように割れも入らない。

1: If you stack plain wood putty, when it dries, it will crack as shown on the left. Instead, dilute wood putty well in water (3 parts to 2-3 parts), add 3 parts of plaster and mix well. This will harden faster than wood putty alone, but allows a longer time to work with than plaster alone. Even after it dries, it will be like stone, with no cracks.

２．ガケの下地に、前記の方法で作ってある。固まるのが速く、カッターや彫刻刀でも簡単に削れる。仕上げに紙粘土を一部使っている。
＊塗装はスポンジとハケで塗ってある。

2: The substrate for the cliffs were made in the way described above. It dries quickly and can easily be shaved with a cutter or sculpting knife. To finish, use papier-mache on parts.
N.B. Paint using a sponge and large brush.

木工パテを溶き、スチロール系の目を潰し、ツルツルに仕上げる
Using Diluted Wood Putty to Cover Lines in Styrol for a Shiny Finish

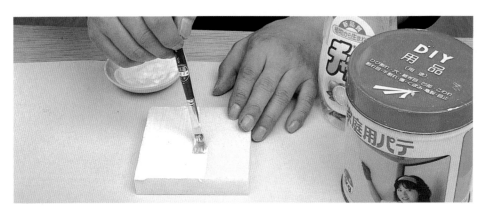

１．木工パテを３、水を１〜２の割合でよく
混ぜる。なかなか混ざり合わなかったら、ラ
ップして一晩寝かせるとよい。筆でパテを塗
り、目を潰す。下地に油分があったりして弾
く場合は、中性洗剤を１滴入れると弾かず伸
びもよい。２度塗りしてから乾かす。

*1: Mix well 3 parts wood putty with 1-2 parts
water. If it won't mix, wrap and let sit
overnight. Apply putty with a brush and
cover lines. If there is oil on the backing or if it
is repelled, add one drop of neutral
detergent and it will go on well without being
repelled. Apply twice and let dry.*

２．急いで乾かす場合、遠くからであればド
ライヤーを使ってもよい。十分乾いたら320番
位のヤスリで削る。キズがあればパテをまた
塗り同じ作業をする。その他の使い方として、
ファンドの補修や先に付け丸くしたりもでき
る。（p.112-14〜16参照）

*2: If you want it to dry quickly, use a dryer
from a distance.
When it dries fully, sand with #320 sandpaper.
If there are any scratches, cover again with
putty and sand. Another method is to repair
with foundation clay or apply to the tip to
round. (See p. 112, 14-16)*

３．600〜1000番のヤスリで仕上げる。左が
木工パテでコーティングされたスチロール。
穴も埋まりエッジもシャープに出る。

*3: To finish, sand with #600-1000 sandpaper.
On the left is styrol coated with wood putty.
The holes are filled and the edges are sharp.*

４．プラモデル用缶スプレーを塗ってみた。
塗料ののりもよく、ツルツルに仕上げられる。
ラッカー系スプレーを塗ると、スチロールが
溶けてしまうので注意。

*4: Here the styrol was painted with spray
paint for plastic models. The paint sticks well,
and the finish is shiny. Do not spray with
lacquer-based paint or the styrol will melt.*

穴やキズを埋める ポリパテの使い方
Filling in Holes and Scratches *Using polyester putty*

1． ABS板やアクリル板などラッカー系パテに強い物であれば、このような穴やキズは、ポリパテで埋めることができる。硬化剤を2～3％の割合でよく混ぜ、へらで押し込むように埋める。

1: If you are using a material resistant to lacquer-based putty such as ABS board or acrylic board, you can fill holes and scratches such as these with polyester putty. Mix well with 2-3% hardener and press in with a spatula.

2． 30～40分で固まる。240番位の耐水ペーパーで削る。ヤスリに水をつければ、目もつまらず早く削れる。

2: It will harden in 30-40 minutes. Sand with approximately #240 waterproof sandpaper. If you apply a little water, you will be able to sand smoothly without getting stuck in the holes.

3． 削るとパテ埋めした部分がヤセてしまうので、タミヤパテをもう一度へらでかぶせるように盛る。＊小さなキズにはタミヤパテが最適である。大きなキズや穴に使うと、中まで固まるのに時間がかかるので注意。タミヤパテはラッカー系なのでスチロール系には使用できない。

3: When sanded, the spots filled with putty will sink, so cover over once more with "Tamiya Putty" using a spatula.
N.B. Tamiya Putty is ideal for small nicks. If used on large scratches or holes, it will take a long time for it to dry on the inside. Tamiya Putty is lacquer-based, so it cannot be used for styrol.

4． 乾いたら600番位のヤスリで削る。タミヤパテはポリパテより粒子が細かいので塗装しても跡が出にくい。

4: When it dries, sand with #600 sandpaper. Tamiya Putty has finer granules than polyester putty, so that even when painted, it will not show through.

 **12**

出ずみを埋める
Filling an Outside Angle

1． ABS板やアクリル板の出ずみの隙間には、ポリパテが最適である。

1: Polyester putty is ideal for the crack on the outside angle of ABS board or acrylic board.

2． ポリパテをへらで、隙間に押し込むようにパテを埋める。

2: Press polyester putty into the crack with a spatula.

3． 平ヤスリ（p.10-1参照）で水をつけながら面に沿って削る。

3: Apply water and sand the surface with a flat file.

4． 隙間だけではなく、面との差もパテ埋めされている。最後にタミヤパテを塗って仕上げると、よりきれいになる。

4: Not only the crack, but the differences in surfaces are filled with putty. Finally apply Tamiya Putty for a cleaner finish.

入りずみを埋める
Filling an Inside Angle

1．ABS板やアクリル板の入りずみの隙間を埋める場合、出ずみのようにパテを多く塗り過ぎると削るのに大変である。そこで‥‥

1: When filling the crack on the inside angle of ABS board or acrylic board, as with the outside angle if too much putty is applied it becomes difficult to file.

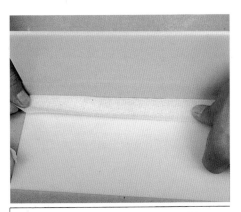

2．隙間のみを残しマスキングテープを貼る。

2: Cover with masking tape, leaving just the crack uncovered.

3．パテをへらで、隙間に押し込むように埋める。

3: Press putty into the crack with a spatula.

4．80°位にカットしたへらで面に沿って引き、余分なパテを取り除く。

4: Using a spatula cut to approximately an 80-degree angle, pull along the surface to remove the excess putty.

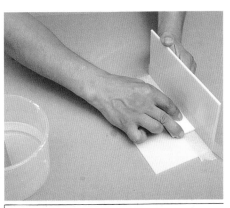

5．20〜30分して固まったら、マスキングテープとの縁を切るためにヤスリをかける。こうしてからテープをはがさないと、テープごとパテが取れてしまうので注意。

5: After it hardens in 20-30 minutes, file to smooth the edge that meets the masking tape. If you do not remove the tape soon, later the putty will come off with the tape when you try to remove it.

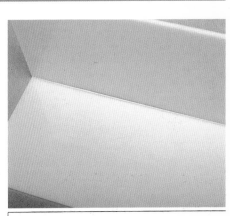

6．テープをはがしてから、軽くヤスリがけして出来上がり。

6: After removing the tape, sand lightly and it will then be complete.

ポリパテに色をつけて
Coloring Polyester Putty

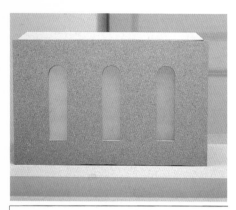

1．仕上げ塗装して組み立てたあとに、隙間を見つけた場合のパテ法である。

1: This is a method for using putty when you discover a crack after the finish painting and assembly has been done.

2．ポリパテを練る時にラッカー塗料を混ぜ、仕上げの色に合わせる。リキテックスでも短時間で混ぜればできる。スチレンペーパーなどは、ポリパテでは溶けてしまうので木工パテにリキテックスを混ぜて作るように。

2: When kneading the polyester putty, mix in lacquer paint and even Liquitex to match the finish color and mix for a short time. Styrene paper will melt if you use polyester putty on it, so use wood putty with Liquitex instead.

3．他の部分を汚さないように、隙間のみを残しマスキングする、パテの埋め方は、入りずみの埋め方と同じ要領で。

3: To make sure not to dirty other parts. Cover with masking tape, leaving only the crack uncovered. Fill with putty in the same manner as for an inside angle.

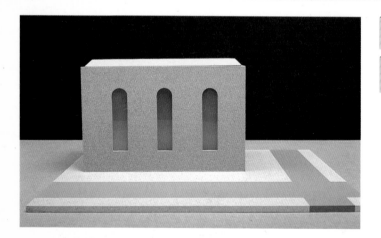

4．隙間に同色のパテを埋めたので、隙間は見えなくなる。

4: Since the crack is filled with putty the same color as the rest of the model, the crack becomes invisible.

大きな円を切ったり書いたりするには 定規を作る
To Cut or Draw a Large Curve *Making a template*

1．規格のコンパスやサークルカッターではとどかない場合、ABS板か厚紙を元太りにカットし、板の中心に直線を書き、元の部分に画鋲で穴をあける。（0点）

1: If a standard compass or circle cutter cannot reach the area to be cut, cut ABS board or thick paper with the base thick, draw a straight line in the center of the board, and open a hole in the base part with a thumbtack. (0 point)

2．半径の寸法を測り、画鋲で穴をあけてから線に直角にカッターを突き刺す。切る厚みまで刃を出す。

2: Measure the radius, and after opening a hole with a thumbtack, cut in a line at a right angle with a cutter. Extend the blade to the depth that will be cut.

3．カッターを引けば切れる。ABS板を切る場合は、切れ目を入れるだけで折れる。

3: When you draw the cutter along, it will cut. When cutting ABS board, just put in a cut line and it will snap off.

4．コンパスとして使う場合は、カッターのかわりにシャープペンシルの先を刺し引けばコンパスのかわりになる。

4: To use as a compass, use a lead pencil instead of a cutter for the tip.

コピーで定規を作る 定規を作る
Making a Template with a Copy *Making a template*

1．定規で印をつけなくても、定規をコピーして裏にスプレーのりをかけ、上に貼ってスコヤで直角を合わせ引くと便利。ここでは6mmピッチのグリッドを引いている。定規を60％に縮小して作れば1cmが6mmになる。

1: Even without making a mark with a template, it is handy to make a copy of the template. Spray glue on the back, paste on top, align at a right angle using a square, and draw. Here, a 6-mm-pitch grid was drawn. By reducing the template 60%, 1-cm becomes 6-mm.

2．大きな物は両はじにコピー定規を貼って使う。

2: For large pieces, paste the copy template onto both edges.

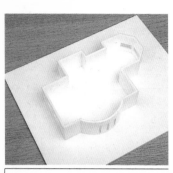

1．このように複雑な形の床に、後ろから床材を貼るのは大変難しい。そこで紙ゲージを作る。

1: For this complex floor shape, it is very difficult to later paste on flooring. For this purpose, create a gauge from paper.

2．腰のある色紙を用意し、スプレーのりを軽くかけ、セーフティベースに貼り四角や台形を切る。曲面はサークルカッターで少し小さめに切り、扇形を作る。下地が白の場合、このように色紙を使うと隙間が見やすい。スプレーのりは、住友3Mの55を使用。

2: Prepare sturdy colored paper, lightly spray on glue, paste onto a safety base and cut the rectangular and trapezoid shapes. Cut the curves with a circle cutter a bit small to create a fan shape. If the backing is white, using colored paper makes extra spaces easy to see. The spray glue used here was 3M 55.

3．紙をコーナーに合わせて重ね貼りしていく。

3: Align the paper with the corner and paste on top.

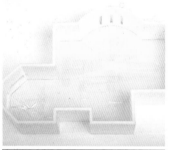

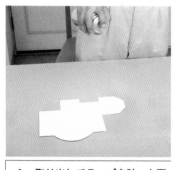

4．曲面に合わせ、扇形の紙を重ね貼っていく。

4: Align with the curve and paste the fan-shaped paper on top.

5．貼れたら、セロハンテープを全面に貼り、ずれないように止める。

5: After these are pasted on, apply cellophane tape to the whole surface to prevent it from sliding.

6．取り出してテープを貼った面にスプレーのりをかける。

6: Remove and spray glue onto the surface where the tape was. N.B. The spray glue used here was 3M 55.

7．床材の裏にのり面を貼り、カッターで形に合わせて切る。表に貼ると、のりが仕上げ面についてしまうので、裏から貼ってある。床材は、ここではジュータンに似たクロス紙を使っている。

7: Paste the surface with glue onto the back side of the floor. Trim the shape with a cutter. If pasted onto the front side, the glue will stick to the finished surface. For flooring, a carpet-like cloth paper was used here.

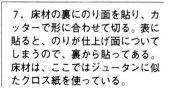

8. R部分は、台紙の端にカッターの刃を合わせて2回で切るとよい。そのためにもゲージにする紙は、厚手のものの方がよい。

8: For the extended part, line up the cutter blade with the edge of the trapezoid and cut twice. For this purpose as well, the paper used as a gauge should be thick.

9. 床材をゲージからはがし、裏にスプレーのりをかける。

9: Peel the flooring from the gauge and spray glue onto the back.

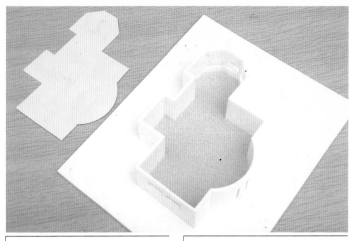

10. 貼って出来上がり。このように隙間なく切り出せる。

10: Paste on and it is done. In this way the floor can be cut without unwanted extra space.

18 一部色違いの床の貼り分け方 床の貼り分け
Pasting on a Floor with Different-Colored Parts Pasting on a floor

1. あらかじめ貼り分ける部分を薄い紙に書くか、17-6で切り出した形を裏からコピーし、それに書き込むとよい。写真中央は、貼り分ける床材。

1: Either draw on thin paper the part to be pasted ahead of time or copy from the back of the shape cut out in Step 6 above and draw onto that. In the middle of the photo is the flooring to be pasted on.

2. 貼り分け材と元の床材の裏から、スプレーのりを軽くかけ、裏向きに3段重ねして貼り、3枚をいっぺんにカットする。

2: Lightly spray glue onto the flooring to be pasted and onto the back of the original flooring. Paste on with the back facing up in three layers and cut all three sheets at once.

3. いったん3枚を取り外し、貼り分け材だけを戻してずれないようにテープで止めておく。最後にもう一度、裏からスプレーのりを十分かける。

3: Temporarily remove all three sheets; put back only the flooring to be pasted on and fix in place with tape so that it does not slip. Finally, spray thoroughly with glue on the back oncemore.

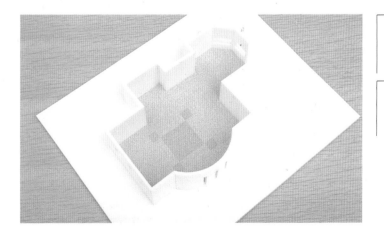

4. コーナーに合わせ、貼ってからテープを取り、出来上がり。この寸法であれば、どんな形でも隙間なく貼り分けられる。

4: Align with the corner, paste on, then remove the tape and it is completed. With this method, you can paste on any shape without unwanted extra space.

お湯で曲げる 曲げる
Bending with Hot Water Bending

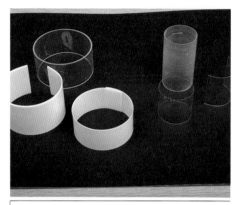

1．1mmのABS板やアクリル板や塩ビ板を曲げるには、曲げたい大きさの筒や缶を用意し、外側に巻き付け、テープでしっかりと止め、90℃位のお湯に1～2分つけておき、取り出して冷ませば曲げられる。厚みが1mm以下の場合は、温度は低めにしておく。

1: To bend 1-mm ABS board, acrylic board or vinyl chloride board, prepare the tube or can of the size you wish to bend the material, wrap around the outside, and hold firmly with tape. Place in approximately 90 degrees water for 1-2 minutes, remove, and when it cools it will bend. If the thickness is less than 1-mm, lower the temperature of the water.

2．2mm位のABS板やアクリル板を曲げるには、戻ろうとする力が強いのでテープで止めることができない。そこで曲げたい大きさの筒に入れ、90～100℃のお湯に2～3分位つける。2mm以上のアクリル板は堅いので、大きめの筒から徐々に曲げたい大きさの筒にかえて、小さくするとよい。

2: When attempting to bend 2-mm ABS board or acrylic board, tape is not strong enough to hold the shape. In this case, place inside a tube of the desired size and place into hot water approximately 90-100 degrees for 2-3 minutes. Acrylic board thicker than 2-mm is rigid, so first bend into a large tube, then change to a smaller tube, gradually reducing the size.

3．右上がゲージの筒。その下は、曲げた透明アクリル0.5mmと1mm。また左上もゲージの筒で、その下が曲げた1mmと2mmのABS板。筒はジュースの缶などを使うとよい。

3: On the upper right is the gauge tube. Below it are 0.5-mm and 1-mm transparent acrylic bent to shape. On the upper left is the gauge tube and below it 1-mm and 2-mm ABS board.

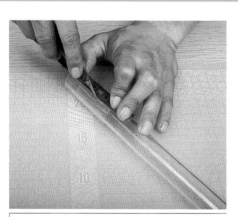

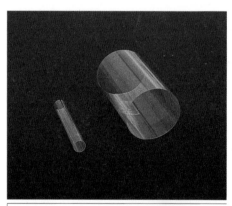

4．小さなRや細いパイプを作るには、ABS板やアクリル板では曲げることは難しい。そこでアセテートフィルムを使って曲げると、3mmφ位まで曲げることができる。丸棒に巻き付け、テープで固定し、90℃位のお湯に20秒位入れて取り出す。

4: It is difficult to use ABS board or acrylic board to make small curves or thin pipes. Instead use acetate film, which can be curved to a diameter of 3-mm. Wrap around a round rod and hold in place with tape. Place in 90 degrees water for about 20 seconds and remove.

5．パイプにして使うには、このように型に巻き付けたまま重なり合った部分を切れば、つなぎ目が合う。

5: If making into a pipe, keep it wrapped around like this, and when you cut the overlapping part, the connecting part will match.

6．左が4mmφの筆の棒に巻き付けたもの。右は20mmφのアクリルパイプに巻き付けたもの。

6: The item on the left was wrapped around a 4-mm diameter brush, and the item on the right was wrapped around an acrylic pipe 20-mm in diameter.

二次曲面のガラス面を作る
Making a Quadratic Glass Surface

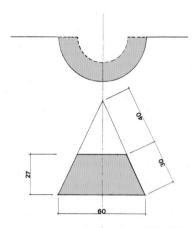

1．このようなガラス面の場合の作り方。

1: How to make this type of glass surface.

2．曲面を図面におこし、寸法を割り出す。ガラス面の延長線の交差点が中心点となる。ここでは黄色の部分を作る。

2: Make a drawing of the curved surface, and calculate the dimensions. The intersection of the extension lines will be the center point of the glass surface. Here we will make the yellow part.

3．サークルカッターで中心からガラスの上の部分を測る。（中心から40mmのところ）

3: Measure the upper part of the glass from the center with the circle cutter. (40-mm from the center)

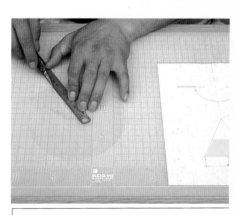

4．アセテートフィルムが切れないように一周する。後で折って切り離すため。

4: Draw all the way around lightly so as not to cut the acetate film. Later you will bend it and break it away.

5．中心から70mmのところ（ガラスの底辺）で切る。

5: Cut at a spot 70-mm from the center (the base of the glass).

6．中心から一部扇状に切り離す。

6: Cut away one part in a fan shape from the center.

7．直径が60mmになるように、中心から巻き込み、テープで止める。この時、中心部を2mm位のポンチで抜いておくと切れたり、割れが入らず巻き込みやすい。

7: So that the diameter becomes 60-mm, wrap from the center and hold with tape. If you put a hole in the center part with a 2-mm hole punch, it will wrap easily without splitting or cracking.

8．75℃位のお湯に40秒位入れ、取り出す。

8: Place into 75 degrees water for 40 seconds and remove.

9．平面に合わせ、カットラインに印をつける。

9: Align with the flat surface and mark for the cut line.

10．印と中心を結び、カットする。

10: Join the mark and the center and cut.

11．4で入れた切れ目を指で折り、切り離す。

11: Bend at the cut line made in Step 4 and break away.

12．出来上がり。

12: The finished piece.

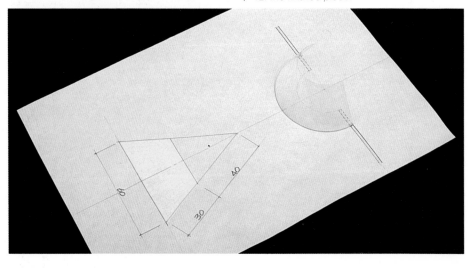

ヒートプレスで曲面を作る 熱加工
Making a Curved Surface with a Heat Press _Heat processing_

1．簡単な熱加工の方法。
半球や円錐、四角錐などの熱加工をするには、まず型になるものを用意するか、木材を使って作る。左はキャップが丸いスプレー缶、右は木材を削り作った四角錐など。

1: A simple heat-processing method. To use heat processing on a hemisphere, circular cone or quadratic cone, first prepare the shape it will be or make it from wood. On the left are spray cans with round caps and on the right are quadratic cones made from carved wood.

2．塩ビ板などを持ちやすいように長めに切り、両端を持ちガスコンロか電気コンロの上にかぶせ、ゆっくり熱する。

2: Cut vinyl chloride board long so that it is easy to hold. Hold both ends, and hold over a gas or electric burner and slowly heat.

3．型を固定し、十分やわらかくなった塩ビ板をかぶせ、下に押し付けると、このように伸びて型通りの形になる。

3: Make sure the form is held solidly, then place the fully softened vinyl chloride board over it, and press down. It will stretch like this into the desired shape.

4．いろいろな型で作ったトップライトやコップなど。左下はABS板1mm、左上は透明アクリル板0.5mm、上は塩ビ板のブラウン0.5mm、右は透明塩ビ板0.5mm。

4: Various toplights and a cup. On the lower left is 1-mm ABS board; on the upper left 0.5-mm transparent acrylic board; Above, brown 0.5-mm vinyl chloride board; and on the right, 0.5-mm transparent vinyl chloride board.

5．p.106のファンドで、スタンドのカサを作る方法と、熱加工でカサを作る方法がある。上のカサは塩ビ板の白をここで紹介した要領で作った。右は、鉄ヤスリでミゾを掘った型で作ったカサ。

5: There are two ways to make lamp shades-- the one shown on p. 106 using foundation clay and this method using heat processing. The lamp shades above were made from white vinyl chloride board using the process described on the previous page. The one on the right was made from a form and the grooves were inserted using a metal file.

熱加工で曲げる
Bending Perpendicular with Heat Processing

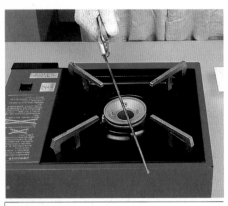  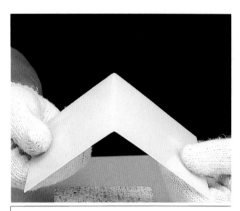

１．市販のヒートがない場合に、このように真鍮棒や鉄、銅などをほどほどに熱する。赤くなるほど熱してはいけない。

1: If an angled piece is not sold in stores, you can make one. Heat up a brass, steel or copper bar. Don't allow it to get redhot.

２．アクリル板やABS板に軽くあて、貼りつくようであれば、熱し過ぎなので少し離す。たれ始めたら棒をあてた側に戻し、曲げる。

2: Lightly press against acrylic board or ABS board. If it starts to stick, the bar is too hot. Hold it a little further away, and when the board begins to sag, pull it back up to the side that the bar has touched and bend.

３．角度を合わせ、固まるまで待つ。

3: Adjust the angle and wait for it to harden.

４．左は２枚折りに曲げたアクリル板。右は90°に曲げたアクリル板。一部を曲げる時は、ハンダゴテを使って曲げるとよい。詳しくはp.66-7～8参照。

4: On the left is acrylic board folded over. On the right is acrylic board bent to a 90-degree angle. When bending just one part, use a soldering iron. For details, see p. 66, 7-8.

白模型用に色を落としたい時 パウダーの色を変える
When Color is Desired for a White Model Changing the color of powder

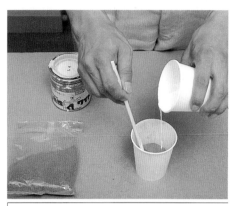

1．市販のパウダーの色が合わない場合色を変える方法。
白模型用に芝用パウダー（シーナリパウダー）を白っぽくしたい場合、白のリキテックスか水性ペイントを水で溶き、パウダーと混ぜる。

1: This is a way to adjust the color of powder if the powder sold in stores is not right. When you want to lighten the color of grass powder (scenery powder) for white models, dilute Liquitex or water-based paint in water and mix with the powder.

2．よくかき混ぜ、厚紙の上に広げて乾かす。

2: Mix well, and spread out on thick paper.

3．1時間おきに広げながら砕く。

3: Every other hour, spread and crush.

4．完全に乾いたら、すり鉢で細かくする。

4: When it dries completely, crush fine with mortar and pestle.

5．左が市販、右が白を入れたもの。2から比べるとかなり元の色に戻っていることに気がつくと思う。すり鉢ですることにより、中の色が外に出るので、色を合わせるには難しい。他の色を混ぜる時は、少量で試してみるとよい。

5: On the left is store-bought powder. On the right is the powder mixed with white, much closer to the original color than in Step 2. When ground with mortar and pestle, the color inside comes out, so matching the color is difficult. When mixing with a different color, it is best to try with a small amount.

6．植え込みの一部に使ってある樹木の丸い玉は、球状の発泡スチロールにプラ棒を刺し、水性塗料を塗ってある。

6: The round balls used for the trees in this model are styrofoam pressed onto plastic rod and painted with water-based paint.

24

缶スプレーの色を混ぜ、中間色にするには 塗る
Mixing Spray Paint Color for an Intermediate Tone *Painting*

1．ぬるま湯に1、2分入れて缶の中の圧力を高め、より細かい霧になるようにしておく。1の色と2の色を交互に塗るか、このように2本いっぺんに50cm位上から左右に振りながらかぶせるように塗ると中間色が出しやすい。

1: Place spray can into hot water for 1-2 minutes to raise the pressure inside the can and make the spray a finer mist. Paint the first and second colors alternately or as shown here, paint both colors at the same time. Spray on from 40-50-cm above, waving left and right to cover. This will bring out an intermediate tone.

2: On the left is a single color, on the right two colors, and in the middle the intermediate color produced from a combination of the two. To make the gradation for the substrate, see p. 76, 29-31.

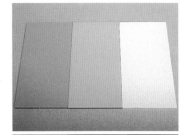

2．左が1の色。右が2の色。中が2本いっぺんに塗った中間色。下地をぼかす方法は p.76-29〜31 参照。

25

缶スプレーの霧を粗くするには
To Enlarge Spray Paint Mist

1．缶スプレーを冷蔵庫に30分位入れて冷やし、缶の中の圧力を低め、粗い粒にして御影石などの塗装に使うとよい。

1: Put the spray can into the refrigerator for about 30 minutes to chill and lower the pressure inside the can. The spray will then be coarser, good for making a marble finish, for example.

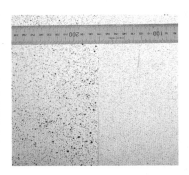

2．右が普通の状態で40cm位離して左右に振りながら吹いたもの。左は冷やした缶スプレーを同じように吹いたもの。ノズルの押し加減でも粒の粗さは変わる。
＊メーカーによってスプレーの出方が変わるので注意。

2: On the right the spraying was done without chilling the can, at a distance of about 40-cm, waving left and right. On the left the same method was used to spray, with a chilled can. Even just by adjusting the amount the nozzle is pressed, the size of the drops will change. N.B. The spray quality will change according to the brand used.

26

絵の具が弾いてしまったら 塗る
When the Paint Does Not Stick *Painting*

1．アクリル板や塩ビ板、スチレンペーパー等にリキテックスなど水性塗料を薄く（水を多めに）ハケ塗りすると、このように弾いてしまうことがある。左はアクリル板、右はスチレンペーパー。

1: When painting Liquitex or other water-based paint thinly (with a lot of water) on acrylic board, vinyl chloride board or styrene paper with a large brush, it sometimes is repelled, as shown here. On the left is acrylic board; on the right is styrene paper.

2．絵の具に1、2滴の中性洗剤を入れ、泡立てないようゆっくり混ぜ、ハケ塗りすればきれいに塗れる。木の染色や板目塗装、大理石の塗装に使う。

2: Add one or two drops of neutral detergent to the paint, mix slowly so as not to raise any bubbles, and it should paint on smoothly with a large brush. Use for tree color, wood grain or marble.

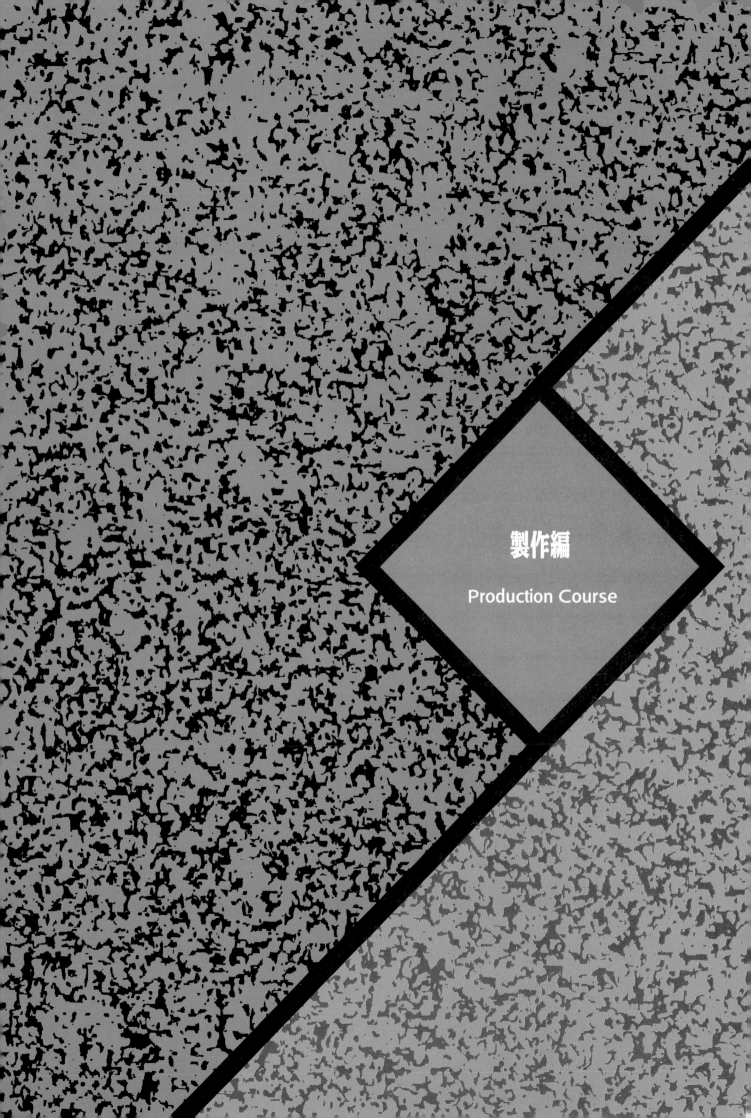

製作編

Production Course

大理石(ティーローズ)の作り方 S=1/50～1/20
How to Make Marble (Tea Rose) S=1/50-1/20

◆使う物：0.3mmアクリル透明板、リキテックス、ティッシュペーパー、アクリルカッター、スチール定規

◆Materials: 0.3-mm acrylic transparent board, liquitex, tissue, acrylic cutter, steel ruler

1．400角の見本。
タイヨー産業(株)TM-001

1:This is a 400-mm square sample. Taiyo Industries TM-001

2．0.3mm～0.5mmの透明アクリル板か、塩ビ板にリキテックスを1.2.3段階の色に調合しておき、1の色(中間色)からティッシュペーパーで軽く押さえる。この時、方向性をつけないように上を塗ったら下と向きを変えながら押さえる。リキテックスは、水を多めにすれば2色目と混ざり合い、大理石の特徴を出しやすい。
＊塩ビ板を使う場合は、少し青味がかっているので色合わせに注意。ティッシュペーパーは、クシャクシャにしてから丸め、十分に塗料を含ませてから押さえるとよい。

2: Apply the liquitex in three stages to adjust the color to a 0.3-mm to 0.5-mm transparent acrylic board or vinyl chloride board. Dab on lightly with a tissue, starting with the first color (intermediate color). So as not to create a directional pattern, apply upwards as well as downwards, changing directions while dabbing. When a little extra water is used, liquitex mixes with the second color and the characteristics of marble are easy to bring out.
N.B. Vinyl chloride board is a little blue-colored, so take this into consideration when matching colors.
Before applying the paint, it is best to crumple the tissue first, then roll it into a ball and soak well in paint.

3．1の色が乾かないうちに、2色目の色を同じようにティッシュペーパーで軽く押さえる。この時、裏が表になるので、裏返して見て2色目が少ないか多すぎないか確かめてみる。1色目が少なかったらもう一度1の色を塗る。

3: Before the first color dries, lightly dab on the second color in the same way. At this time, turn it over and make sure that the there is not too little or too much of the second color, because the back becomes the front. If there is not enough of the first color reapply the first color.

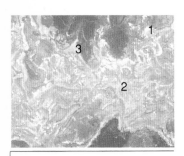

4．続けて3の色を軽く押さえるように塗る。ここでもう一度、完全に乾かす。(ドライヤーを使う場合は遠くからあてる)

4: Next, apply the third color with light pressure. After doing so, let it dry thoroughly (If you use a dryer, use it from a distance).

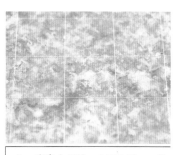

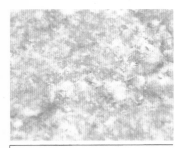

5．隙間が埋まるまで、1～3の色を繰り返し塗れば出来上がり。

5: Repeat the application of colors 1-3 until there are no more gaps; then the coloring is finished.

6．そのままではスケール感がないので、グリッドを入れてみる。アクリルカッターで目地をけがく、ここでは400角の1/20で、20mmピッチに入れてみた。色目地にしたい場合は、リキテックスの原液を筆で目地に満遍なく埋める。

6: Since there is no sense of scale at this point, try putting in a grid. Using an acrylic cutter, put in joints. Working here at a scale of 1/20 in a 400-mm square, we have put in the joints at a 20-mm pitch. If you want to color the joints, apply undiluted liquitex with a paint brush, leaving no lines uncovered.

7．乾かないうちにティッシュペーパーで拭き、拭き残しはアルコールを浸したティッシュペーパーで斜め方向に軽く拭き取る。グリッドに沿って拭くと、溝の中のリキテックスをえぐり出してしまうので注意。

7: Before it dries, wipe with a tissue, and whatever remains wipe away lightly using a tissue soaked in alcohol in a diagonal direction. If you wipe along the grid lines, the liquitex in the grooves will get scooped out.

8．出来上がり。1マス20mmの目地である。ここでは目地の色はベージュにしてある。

8: The finished model. One square of the grid is 20-mm per side. Here the joints are colored beige.

大理石(ロッソベローナ)の作り方 S＝1/50〜1/20
How to Make Marble (Rosso Verona) S=1/50-1/20

◆使うもの：0.3mmアクリル透明板、タオル、リキテックス、筆　　◆Materials: 0.3-mm acrylic transparent board, towel, liquitex, paint brush

1．これが実物の写真。ADV SIC 4447

1: This is a photo of the actual marble. ADV SIC 4447

2．タオルを小さく切り、リキテックスを含ませ乗せるように中間色から塗る。

2: Cut a towel into small pieces, soak in liquitex and apply by placing on, starting with the intermediate color.

3．濃いめの茶色を塗ってから白系を乗せる。

3: First apply the darker brown and then lay on the white lines.

4．石の特徴である流れるような白をだすために筆で白を塗る。

4: To bring out the flowing white characteristics of the stone, apply white with a paint brush.

5．白が乾かないうちにタオルでなじませる。

5: Before the white dries, use a towel to spread.

6．出来上がり。
タオルの目の丸い模様がティッシュペーパーとは違う表現になる。

6: The finished model. The wavy pattern that a towel texture creates is different from that made using tissue.

3

テラゾーの作り方 テラゾーをスポンジタワシで作る
How to Make Terazzo S=1/50-1/20 Making terazzo with a sponge brush

1．これが実物の写真。
ADV MCA615

1: This is a picture of genuine terazzo. ADV MCA615

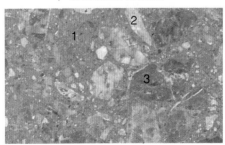

2．透明アクリル板か塩ビ板の0.3mmにリキテックスで1〜3の色を調合したものを、スポンジタワシのタワシ部分を使って軽く押さえる。
＊タワシにリキテックスをつけ過ぎるとAのように大きくなり、スポンジを上げる時に手首を回してしまうと、Bのように円になるので注意する。

2: Apply three liquitex colors to 0.3-mm thick transparent acrylic board or vinyl chloride board lightly dabbing on with the brush part of a sponge brush.
N.B. If you get too much liquitex on the brush it will look as pictured in A. Slightly turning your wrist when raising the sponge will help to create circular pattern.

◆使う物：0.3mmアクリル透明板、リキテックス、スポンジタワシ
◆Materials: 0.3-mm acrylic transparent board, liquitex, sponge brush

3．1の色の上に2を乗せる。3の色も同じように塗り、裏返して確かめ少ない色を重ねて塗る。

3: Put the second color on top of the first. Apply the third color in the same way, turn it over to check, and apply on top any color that is insufficient.

4．裏返して色味が違った場合、色味が合う色を作り全体的にハケ塗りすれば、多少色が変わる。例えば、白すぎた場合こげ茶色を塗れば茶色に近づく。この時、下塗りが十分乾いてからハケ塗りをしないと、色が流れてしまうので注意する。

4: Turn the board over, and if the tone is not right, create a color that matches the tone. By brushing the entire surface, the color can be changed slightly. For example, if it is too white, apply dark brown and it will become brown. If the under layers are not fully dry, however, when you brush on the paint, the colors will run.

5．出来上がり。スケール感を出すためにグリッドをアクリルカッターで入れる。
＊タオルとはまた違った表現になる。

5: The finished model. To bring out the sense of scale, use the acrylic cutter to cut in a grid.
N.B. A different feel is created here than when using a towel.

---

4 大理石(キャンティーマーブル)の作り方
大理石(キャンティーマーブル)を中性洗剤を使って作る

How to Make Marble (Chianti Marble)
Making Chianti marble using a neutral detergent

◆使う物：0.3mmアクリル透明板、リキテックス、筆、中性洗剤

◆Materials: 0.3-mm acrylic transparent board, liquitex, paint brush, neutral detergent

1．これが実物の写真。ADV BEN6207

1: This is a photo of genuine Chianti marble. ADV BEN 6207

2．リキテックスを薄めに溶き、中性洗剤を1、2滴加え、軽く混ぜる（p.28-26参照）。平筆に中間色をたっぷり含ませた後で平筆の端に少し濃い色をつけ塗る。

2: Dilute the liquitex with water to make it rather thin, then add 1-2 drops of neutral detergent and mix lightly (See p. 28-26). Soak a flat paint brush thoroughly in the intermediate color, then dip the tip of the pen in a slightly darker color, and apply.

3．2で塗った後、裏返してみて濃い色が多ければ白系の色だけを乾かないうちに塗り合わせる。白が多ければ濃い色を塗る。

3: Next, turn the board over. If the dark color is too thick, apply only a white before it dries to balance it out. If there is too much white, apply the dark color.

4．出来上がり。

4: The finished model.

5．そのままではスケール感がないので400角の1/20で20mm四方の貼り分けをしてみる。カットの仕方、貼り方はp.37-9参照。

5: Since there is no sense of scale at this point, try putting in a 20-mm square grid, 1/20 the scale of the 400-mm square. For how to cut and paste, see p. 37-9.

白御影石の作り方
How to Make White Granite

◆使う物：0.3mmアクリル透明板、リキテックス、4mmピッチの金網、歯ブラシ、白のプラモデル用缶スプレー

◆Materials: 0.3-mm acrylic transparent board, liquitex, 4-mm pitch wire screen, toothbrush, white spray paint for plastic models

1．実物の写真。水磨き仕上げで表面がツルツルである。ADV AG 8417

1: This is a photo of genuine white marble. Its water-rubbed finish is shiny. ADV AG 8417

3．グレーが乾いたら白をブラシにつけ、網にブラシをこすりつける。

3: After the gray has dried, apply white to the brush and rub it across the screen.

2．0.3mmの透明アクリル板か塩ビ板と、持ちやすい大きさに切った3〜4mm角ピッチの金網と歯ブラシを用意する。リキテックスの黒、白、グレー、シルバーを濃いめに溶いておく。はじめに白い紙の上に置いた透明板の上で、歯ブラシにグレーをつけ網にブラシをこすりつける。グレーの丸い粒が飛ぶが、やりすぎないように注意する。

＊塗る前に透明板をティッシュペーパーにアルコールか水をつけて拭き、静電気を取ってから塗るように。

2: Prepare transparent acrylic board or vinyl chloride board, 3 or 4-mm square pitch wire screen cut into an easy-to-hold piece and a toothbrush. Dilute black, white, gray and silver liquitex a little, keeping it slightly thick. First place the transparent board on top of white paper. Apply gray to the toothbrush and rub across the screen held above the board. Round, gray drops will spray around, so use moderation.
N.B. Before applying, wipe the transparent board with a tissue dipped in alcohol or water to remove static electricity.

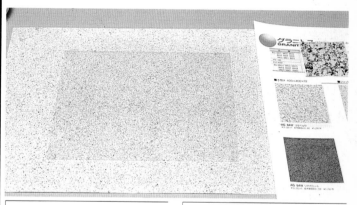

4．次に黒を塗った後、シルバーも塗る。少ない色がある場合は塗り足してやる。

＊前に塗った色が乾いてから次の色を塗れば、塗り過ぎてぼた落ちした場合でもティッシュペーパーで押さえればその部分だけ拭き取れる。

4: Next, apply the black and then the silver. If there is not enough of one color, add more of it.
N.B. When a color is applied after the previous color has dried, if a large amount drops accidentally or if too much is applied, that part alone can be dabbed off with a tissue.

7．円の白御影石と黒御影石を1枚の板で作ってみる。7で塗った面にマスキングシートなどで全体的にマスキングをし、サークルカッターで円に切り、円の部分だけを残し、あとははがす。そこに黒の缶スプレーを満遍なく塗り、乾いたら円のマスキングシートをはがし白を塗る。1枚の透明板に2色の石が作れる。この方法で市松模様などを作ってみるのもよい。

7: Try making one board that has both round white granite and black granite. Cover the board painted in Step 7 entirely with a masking sheet, use a circle cutter to cut a circle, and leave the sheet on the circle part. Remove the rest. Spray with black paint, and after it has dried thoroughly, remove the masking sheet. When white is applied, two colors of stone can be created on one transparent board. Using this method, it is also good to try making a checkerboard pattern.

5．プラモデル用缶スプレーの白で、仕上げ塗りをする。黒御影石の場合は、黒の缶スプレーを塗ればよい。

5: Create the finish using white spray paint for plastic models. For black granite use black spray paint.

6．裏返したら白御影石の出来上がり。（拡大したところ）

6: When you turn it over, it should look like white granite (A detail is shown here).

6 御影石のジェットバーナー仕上げの作り方
How to Make Granite with a Torched Finish

◆使う物：0.3mmアクリル板、スポンジタワシ、金網、歯ブラシ、平筆、リキテックス

◆Materials: 0.3-mm acrylic board, sponge brush, wire screen, toothbrush, flat paint brush, liquitex

1．実物の写真。ザラザラな表面に小さな黒、シルバーが入っているのに注意。

1: This is a photo of the genuine item. Notice the small amounts of black and silver mixed in with the large part.

2．ツルツルの表面を作るには、透明板の裏から着色するが、ジェットバーナー仕上げのようなザラザラの面は表から色を重ねる。まず本物の石をよく観察し、全体のトーンより薄めの色を作って平筆で縦横に重ね塗りする。

2: To make the surface shiny, you would add color on the reverse side of the transparent board, but to get the coarse torched finish, one must add color to the surface. First, closely examine the real stone, then create a slightly lighter overall tone, and paint on with a flat brush using vertical and horizontal strokes.

3．ハケ塗りの表面が乾いたら、白系の色からタワシ部分を使って軽く押しつけるように塗る。塗料は少し濃いめにするとザラザラ感が出しやすい。

3: After the brush-painted surface dries, apply color starting with white. Lightly dab on with the brush part of the sponge brush. Using slightly thick paint makes it is easy to bring out the coarseness.

4．前の塗料が乾いたら、中間色位の茶を塗る。

4: When the previous layer of paint has dried, apply an intermediate brown color.

5．少し白を混ぜた色で同様に塗る。

5: Apply color mixed with a little white in the same way.

6．また白系を塗り重ねる。

6: Paint white over this.

7．次に濃いめの茶色を塗る。このような色の違いを重ねることにより、微妙な色の違いや表面の凹凸が忠実に再現できる。そのためには各色を違う皿に多めに作っておかなければならない。

7: Next apply a darker brown. By painting on different layers of color in this way, fine differences in color and a raised surface can be faithfully reproduced. For this purpose, a generous amount of each color must be kept in separate trays.

8．リキテックスのシルバーを水で溶き、歯ブラシにつけて3～4mmピッチの金網にこすりつけてまきちらす。

8: Dilute silver liquitex with water, apply to the toothbrush and brush across a 3 to 4-mm pitch wire screen to splatter fine drops.

9．シルバーと同じ要領で黒もまきちらす。

9: Splatter black in the same manner as the silver.

10．出来上がり。

10: The finished model.

11．拡大写真。

11: A detail is shown here.

丸柱などの曲面に大理石模様の塗り方
丸柱などの曲面に大理石の水磨き仕上げ風塗装をする

How to Paint a Marble Pattern on Round Columns and Other Curved Surfaces
Painting a rubbed marble finish on an entire column or curved surface

◆使う物：リキテックス、ティッシュペーパー、面相筆、クリヤー缶スプレー　　◆Materials: liquitex, tissue, fine brush, clear spray paint

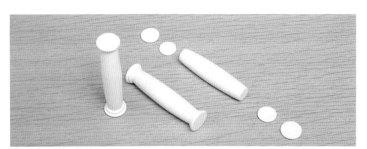

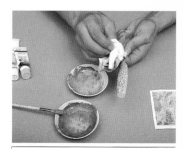

1．このような曲面には、アクリル板などで作った材料を巻き付けることは不可能である。そこで従来の製作工程の逆から作る。この丸柱はスタイロフォームを木工パテでコーティングしてある。作り方は p.123〜124 参照。

1: With this type of curvature, it is impossible to wrap a material made from acrylic board. A completely different approach must therefore be used. This round column is made of styrofoam with a wood putty coating. See p. 123-124 for how to make it.

2．中間色をプラモデル用缶スプレーで各パーツごとに下地塗りする。写真下の2種類の石を塗ってみるので、お互いに共通の色、ベージュを塗ってみた。

2: Use an intermediate color of spray paint for plastic models for painting the substrate of each part. In the picture below, two types are stone have been painted, both with a beige color.

3．テイッシュペーパーにグレーを含ませ、軽く押さえるように塗る。一度に塗りつぶさないように注意する。

3: Soak the tissue in gray, and dab on, pressing lightly. Be careful not to press too hard so as not to apply too much at once.

4．茶と白を同じように塗る。色が合うまで繰り返す。
＊微妙に混ざり合った感じを出すため、テイッシュペーパーは色ごとに変える必要はない。

4: Apply both brown and white in the same way. Repeat the process until the color matches the intended color.
N.B. Do not change the tissue for each color. Use the same tissue to bring out a fine mixture.

5．テイッシュペーパーで出せなかった模様は、面相筆で模様を書く。

5: Draw on with a fine brush the pattern that could not be made with the tissue.

6．台座も同じ要領で塗る。

6: Paint the pedestal in the same manner.

7．乾いたら柱と台座をスチのりで接着し、柱を角材に両面テープで固定し塗りやすくする。クリヤーの缶スプレーを全体的に塗り、一度乾かしてからもう一度塗る。
＊スタイロフォームやスチレンペーパーの下地は、ラッカー系を塗ると溶けてしまうので注意する。ここではプラモデル用クリヤーを使った。

7: When everything is dry, attach the column and the pedestal using styrene glue. If you hold the column to a block of wood it will be easier to paint. Use a clear spray paint and spray on over the entire piece. When it dries, spray once more.
N.B. Do not use lacquer-based paint, which will melt styrofoam and styrene paper. Use clear spray for plastic models instead.

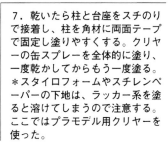

8．出来上がり、クリヤーを塗ることにより水磨き仕上げのような光沢が出る。

8: The finished model. When clear spray is applied, the luster of a water-rubbed finish is achieved.

ジェットバーナー仕上げの市松模様の作り方

御影石のジェットバーナー
仕上げと本磨き仕上げの
市松模様を作ってみる

How to Make a Checkerboard Pattern with Torched Finish

Making a checkerboard pattern with torched and polished granite finish

◆使う物：0.3mmアクリル透明板、リキテックス、金網、歯ブラシ、マスキングシート、缶スプレー（グレー、黒、ツヤ消しクリヤー）

◆Materials: 0.3-mm acrylic transparent board, liquitex, wire screen, toothbrush, masking sheet, spray paint (gray, black, flat clear)

1．同じ黒御影石に「本磨き仕上げ」と「ジェットバーナー仕上げ」を施し、両者を市松模様に貼り分けた例を模型で再現してみよう。まずp.33の白御影石の要領で、本磨き仕上げの黒御影石を作る。初めに金網と歯ブラシを用いてアクリル板に、リキテックスのグレー、白、シルバーをまきちらす。

1: Using the same black granite, let's try reproducing in the model a tiled checkerboard pattern both in a polished finish and torched finish. First, in the same manner as with the white granite on p. 33, make black granite with a polished finish. First splatter gray, white and silver liquitex on the acrylic board by rubbing the toothbrush across the wire screen.

2．1が乾いたらこの上に黒のプラモデル用缶スプレーをむらなく吹き付ける。

2: When the paint in Step 1 is dry, spray on black plastic model spray paint thoroughly.

3．乾いた2を裏返すと、黒御影石の本磨き仕上げになる。

3: When the paint applied in Step 2 is dry, turn the board over and you have a polished finish for the black granite.

4．次にマスキングシートを全面に貼る。

4: Next, stick the masking sheet onto the entire board.

5．シートの上からカッターで、本磨き仕上げとジェットバーナー仕上げの境界線に当たる部分に切れ目を入れる。コピー定規を使うと便利。（p.19-16参照）

5: With the cutter, cut from the top of the sheet to mark the border of the polished finish and torched finish, putting in a groove. Using a copy ruler makes this process easy (See p. 19-16).

6．本磨きのツルツルした面は、マスキングシートをそのまま残し、ジェットバーナー仕上げの部分だけマスキングシートをはがす。

6: Leave the masking sheet on the shiny polished finish surface, and remove it only for the torched finish part.

7．次に濃いグレーの缶スプレーを50cm位離して、左右に振りながら吹きちらす。次に、黒も同じ要領で吹き付け、最後にツヤ消しクリヤーを塗る。
＊缶スプレーは、べた塗りせず、ふわっとかけるのがコツ。塗り過ぎに注意。

7: Next, hold a can of dark gray spray paint at a distance of about 50-cm and spray in a swinging motion left and right. Then spray on black in the same manner. N.B. The key is to spray on lightly. Be careful not to get it too wet.

8．残りのマスキングシートを、全部はがせばご覧の通りのツルツルとザラザラの市松模様の貼り分けた床材の出来上がり。

8: Remove all of the remaining masking sheet and as you see, a flooring pattern of shiny and coarse checkerboard tiles has been created.

石のパターン貼りの作り方
How to Make a Stone Pattern Veneer

出来上がった4種類の石の模型材料を使って
インテリアを組み立てる

Assembling the interior using the four types of stone model materials you have made.

◆使う物：スプレーのり、アクリルカッター、スチール定規、カッター

◆Materials: spray glue, acrylic cutter, steel ruler, cutter

1．4種類の石の模型材料を模型の縮小率に従って切り分ける。ここでは400mm角の石材を床と壁の一部に貼った1/20スケールの模型を作るから、20mm角が必要になる。まずスチール定規をあて、アクリルカッターで20mm間隔のグリッドをV溝にけがく。コピー定規を使うと便利。(p.19-16参照)

1: Cut the four types of stone model materials according to scale. Here you will make a 1/20 scale model with 400-mm square stone material for the floor and part of the wall, so 20-mm squares are needed. First, use the acrylic cutter braced against the steel ruler to cut in a V-groove grid at 20-mm intervals. Using a copy ruler makes this process easy (See p. 19-16).

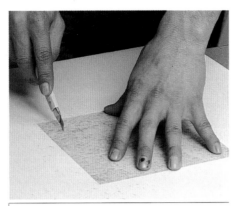

2．今度は普通のカッターで、1でつけた溝に沿って軽く切り込みを入れる（定規は不要）。これをしないと後で1枚ずつ割りにくいため。

2: Then, using an ordinary cutter, lightly slice along the groove made in Step 1 (no ruler needed). If you do not do this, it is difficult to break apart later.

3．裏にスプレーのりを満遍なく吹き付ける。30cm位離して吹き、半乾きになったらもう一度吹く。この後切れ目に沿って折ると、簡単にバラバラになる。

3: Spray glue thoroughly onto the reverse side. Spray at a distance of about 30-cm. When it is half-dry, spray once more. Then break along the grooves to separate easily into pieces.

4．切り離した各材料を腰のある紙に貼っていく。白大理石のように石目がある場合は、写真のように「目」の向きを交互に組み合わせていくと本物らしく見える。馴れないうちは下地にグリッドを書いておき、ずれてきたらそのつどカッターで切って修正するとよい。

4: Paste the cut-up materials onto sturdy paper. If there is a grain, as with white marble, arrange alternately with the grain, as shown in the picture to make it look like the real thing. Until you get good at doing this, draw in a grid on the backing and if it shifts, cut each time with the cutter to fix.

5．完成した石貼りのインテリア。床、壁、腰の下地はスチレンペーパーを使ってある。壁はケント紙につや消しホワイトの缶スプレーを吹きつけスプレーのりで貼ってある。窓ガラスは透明アクリル板につや消しクリヤーを吹き付けてある。

5: The finished stone veneer interior.The floor, walls and sturdy backing are made from styrene paper. For the walls, a flat white is sprayed onto Kent paper and fixed on with spray glue. For the window glass, flat clear paint is sprayed onto transparent acrylic board.

コンクリートの作り方
塩ビ板を使ってコンクリート床を作ってみる

How to Make Concrete
Creating a concrete floor using vinyl chloride board

◆使う物：0.3〜0.5mmの塩ビ板、缶スプレー（グレー、白、黒）、紙ヤスリ

◆Materials: 0.3 to 0.5-mm vinyl chloride board, spray paint (gray, white, black), sandpaper

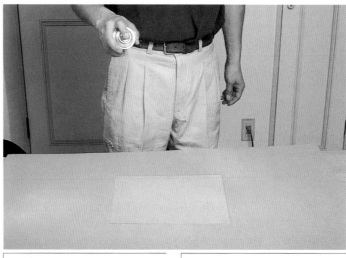

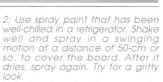

1．まず塩ビ板に塗料が乗りやすいように紙ヤスリ（240番位）を縦横にかける。塩ビ板の他に紙でもできるが、床を作る場合は塩ビ板の方が、ジョイント目地を入れた時きれいに出る。壁を作るなら紙でも十分である。

1: First, to make the vinyl chloride board easy to paint, rub it with sandpaper both vertically and horizontally. Use sandpaper #240 or so. Concrete can also be made from paper, but for flooring, vinyl chloride board appears nicer when joints are put in. For walls, paper is sufficient.

2．グレーの缶スプレーでまんべんなく塗り乾いたら白の缶スプレーを冷蔵庫でよく冷やしてからよくふり、50cmぐらい離して左右にふりながら、かぶせるように吹きつける。ザラつかせるのがコツ。
＊歯ブラシと金網を使ってもよい。（p.33- 2 〜 4 参照）

2: Use spray paint that has been well-chilled in a refrigerator. Shake well and spray in a swinging motion at a distance of 50-cm or so, to cover the board. After it dries, spray again. Try for a gritty look.
N.B. It is also okay to use a wire screen and toothbrush (see p. 33-2~4), but here try making it with spray paint.

3．続いて黒・グレーの順でスプレーをかける。黒は目立つためほんの一瞬かけるだけでよい。失敗しても、もう一度グレー、白、黒の順でスプレーし直せば大丈夫。

3: Then apply black spray paint. Since black stands out, spray for just an instant. If you make a mistake, you can respray on gray, white, and black in that order to fix it.

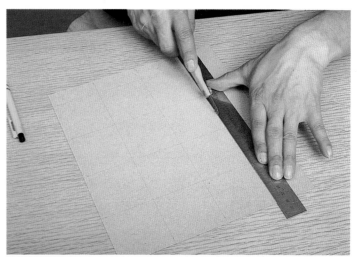

4．出来上がり。

4: The finished model.

5．アクリルカッターで、ジョイント目地を引いてみる。紙ではこのような目地は入れられないので、床の場合はアクリル板か塩ビ板を使うのがよい。

5: With an acrylic cutter, try cutting in the joints. With paper you cannot put in joints like this, so for flooring it is best to use acrylic board or vinyl chloride board.

コンクリート打ち放し仕上げ

打ち放しは、目地を入れた厚紙に
ポンチで穴をあけて

How to Make an Exposed Concrete Finish

The exposed finish is made by punching
holes in thick paper that has joints in it

◆使う物：グレー系の紙2色、カッター、スチール定規、ポンチ、金づち、スプレーのり

◆Materials: gray paper in two colors, cutter, steel ruler, hole puncher, hammer, spray glue

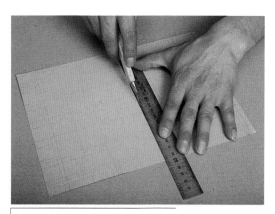

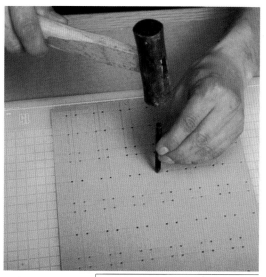

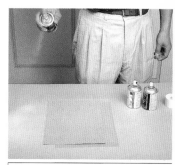

1．薄いグレーのカラーケント紙を実物のコンパネ板のサイズに合わせ鉛筆でグリットをひく、そのあとで打ち放しコンクリート特有のコーン穴になるところにも、しるしをつける。カッターでグリットに合わせ縦横に合板の目地を入れる。切れない程度に軽く。

1: According to a scale of the actual concrete panel grid, use the cutter to cut gray paper (colored card) in vertical and horizontal strokes for the plywood joints. Cut very, very lightly. Then mark with a pencil the places that will be the special holes of plain concrete.

2．そこをポンチで穴をあけていく。今回使ったポンチは直径 1.2 mmのもの。

2: Open the holes using a hole puncher. The diameter of the holes this time should be 1.2-mm.

3．鉛筆のしるしを消してから白、黒、グレーの順で塗装する。（グレーの紙なのでグレーの下塗りはいらない。）

3: After erasing the pencil marks, paint the concrete in the same way as you did with the concrete flooring.

4．乾いたら裏返してスプレーののりをかけ、それを濃いめのグレーの紙に貼る。

4: When it dries, turn it over and spray on the glue. Then paste on dark gray paper.

5．曲面に使う時は、折る溝にもう一度カッターで下の台紙に刃が届く位切り込みを入れると、このように曲げることができる。

5: When using it for curved surfaces, once more cut with the cutter in the fold groove and cut until the blade just about reaches the mount paper. This allows you to bend the paper.

6．この材料を使ってインテリアを組み立ててみた。壁などに使う場合、木工ボンドを使うとシワになったり反ってしまうので、スプレーのりの55か77を使うことを薦める。中央のコンクリート丸柱は、アクリルパイプに缶スプレーでコンクリート塗装してある。

6: The interior has been assembled here using these materials. If using for walls, for example, spray-on glue 55-77 is recommended over wood bond, which forms wrinkles or will warp the paper. The central concrete column is made of acrylic pipe sprayed with concrete paint.

コンクリートブロックの作り方 コンクリートブロックは全体的に白っぽく

How to Make Concrete Blocks *Making generally white-colored concrete blocks*

◆使う物：グレーの塩ビ板0.5mm、缶スプレー（グレー、白、ダークグレー）、アクリルカッター、スチール定規

◆Materials: gray 0.5-mm vinyl chloride board, spray paint (gray, white, dark gray), acrylic cutter, steel ruler

1．コンクリートブロックは、普通のコンクリートに比べると、表面が白っぽい。そこでまずグレーの塩ビ板に、白の缶スプレーを50cm位離してザラザラになるように2、3回塗る。
＊歯ブラシと金網を使ってもよい。

1: The surface of concrete blocks are whiter than ordinary concrete. First, spray white paint at a distance of 50-cm onto gray vinyl chloride board two or three times to create a coarse texture.
N.B. It is also okay to use a wire screen and toothbrush.

2．次にダークグレーの缶スプレーを50cm位離し振りながら、サッとかける。次に白とグレーで色を合わせる。

2: Next, use dark gray, hold 50-cm away and spray just a bit with a wave of the hand. Follow this with white and gray to build the right color.

3．こんな感じに仕上げればよい。この方法は白御影石のジェットバーナー仕上げにも使える。

3: Finish so that it looks somewhat like this. This method can also be used for a white granite torched finish.

4．乾いたらアクリルカッターで目地を入れる。

4: When it dries, cut in the joints using an acrylic cutter.

5．表面塗装が削り取られ、グレーの塩ビ板が出るので、このようにコンクリート目地のようになる。

5: Scrape off the paint on the surface to reveal the gray vinyl chloride board underneath. This is how the concrete joints are made.

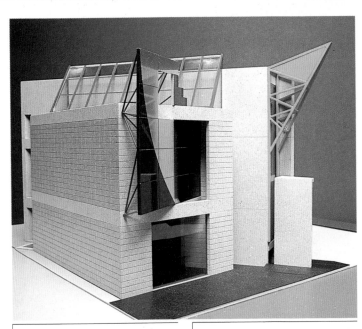

6．ここに紹介したカラーブロックは、目地の深さを変えて、荒れた感じを出している。このブロックの目地は、ブロックと同色なので目地を入れてから塗装してある。

6: By changing the depth of the joints on the colored blocks introduced here, a coarser texture is produced. Since the joints on these blocks are the same color as the blocks themselves, painting is done after the joints are cut out.

13

タイルの作り方 黒目地で表面が白いタイルを作ってみる
How to Make Tiles *Making white tiles with black joints*

◆使う物：黒の塩ビ板、白の缶スプレー、紙ヤスリ、アクリルカッター、スチール定規

◆Materials: black vinyl chloride board, white spray paint, sandpaper, acrylic cutter, steel ruler

1．目地が黒だから、まず黒の塩ビ板0.3か0.5mm厚を用意する。塗料の食いつきをよくするために紙ヤスリをかける。

1: Because the joints are to be black, first prepare a vinyl chloride board that is 0.3-mm or 0.5-mm thick. So that the paint sticks well, first rub the board with sandpaper.

2．次に白の缶スプレーを満遍なくベッタリかける。乾いたらもう一度塗る。半ツヤの場合は、遠くからもう一度かけるか、ツヤ消しの白かツヤ消しクリヤーを軽くかける。

2: Next, plaster the board thoroughly with white spray paint. When it dries, paint again. If the paint is semigloss, either spray it on from a distance of use flat white. Flat clear can also be sprayed on lightly instead.

3．乾いたらアクリルカッターでタイル目地を入れる。

3: When it dries, use an acrylic cutter to make the tile joints. Use a copy ruler .

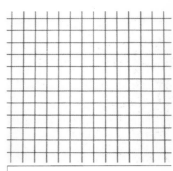

4．出来上がり。

4: The finished work.

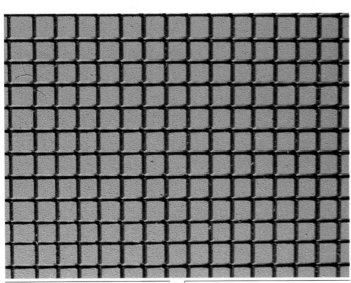

5．茶のタイルに黒の目地、2mm角のモザイクタイルの拡大。（黒の塩ビ板0.3mm使用）

5: This is an enlargement of brown 2-mm mosaic tiles with black joints (using 0.3-mm black vinyl chloride board).

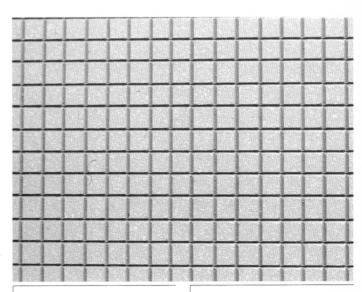

6．ピンクのタイルにグレーの目地。（グレーの塩ビ板0.3mm使用）

6: Gray joints on pink tiles (using 0.3-mm gray vinyl chloride board).

クラックタイルの作り方 白の磁器タイルをクラックにして
How to Make Tiles with Cracks *Making white porcelain tiles with cracks*

◆使う物：白の紙（LKカラー）、グレーの紙（カラーケント）、カッター、スチール定規、スプレーのり

◆Materials: white paper (LK Color), gray paper (kent paper), cutter, steel ruler, spray glue

1．表面がツルツルした紙（LKカラー）を用意する。（これより薄いルミナカラーがあるから、模型が小さい場合はこれを使うとよい）タイルの色の紙がない場合は、缶スプレーで色を合わせてもよい、まず裏返してスプレーのりをかける、住友3M 55使用。

1: Use shiny paper (LK Color) for the surface (Lumina Color paper is thinner, which is good for small models). If there is no paper the color of the tile, use spray paint to adjust the color. First turn it over and apply spray glue. 3M 55 was used here.

2．それを下敷きに張りつけて、カッターでマス目（正方形）に切る。出来上がりは30mm角だが、それはクラックを入れた大きさだからマス目は一まわり小さい28mm角にしておく。

2: Paste this onto the backing, and cut precise squares with the cutter. The finished tile size will be 30-mm square, but that includes the cracks, so make the squares a drop smaller at 28-mm.

3．一マスごとにクラックを入れるのは大変なので、マス目3～4個分ずつをごく大ざっぱにカットする。クラックだから線を規則的につけないように。

3: It is too much trouble to put in a crack for every square one by one, so cut roughly for every 3 to 4 squares. Since they are cracks, make sure the lines are not too straight.

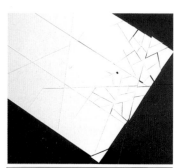

4．さらに細かいクラックを入れていく。次にタイルの台紙となるグレーの紙（カラーケント）を用意する。台紙にはあらかじめ30mm角の目地を入れておく。

4: Then put in fine cracks one by one. Next, prepare the gray paper (kent paper) that will serve as the tile mount. Put in 30-mm square joints in the mount ahead of time.

5．この台紙に先程の下敷きからはがしたものを、マスごとに貼る。マスの位置はカットしたマスの位置と変えるのがコツ。ここでは意匠としてグリッド目地にステンレス棒が入っているから、台紙には目地に沿ってシルバーの粘着テープ（レトラテープ）を貼ってそれらしく見せた。

5: Paste onto each square of this mount what you removed previously from the backing. The key to the positioning of the squares is in shifting them from their original position. The design here calls for stainless steel bar in the grid joints, so apply sticky adhesive tape along the joints to represent the piping.

6．出来上がり。

6: The finished work.

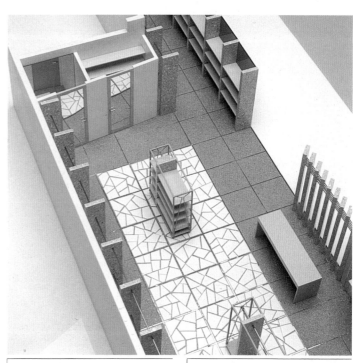

7．木の棚や什器は、ABS板で作ってある。

7: The wood shelves and cabinet are made of ABS board.

乱貼りの作り方
How to Make Staggered Veneer

◆使う物：薄い紙、缶スプレー、スポンジタワシ、リキテックス、スプレーのり、カッター

◆Materials: thin paper, spray paint, sponge brush, liquitex, spray glue, cutter

ADV KZCQ 1030

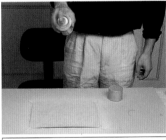

1．実物の石の写真。

1: This is a photo of the real stone.

2．石の下地の色に近いグレーの紙を用意する（ここではグレーの缶スプレーで下地の色を塗った）。紙の収縮を押さえるためコーナーをテープで止め、スポンジタワシのタワシ部分に茶色のリキテックスを含ませ、押さえるように塗る。

2: Prepare gray paper that is close in color to the base of the stone (Here, gray spray paint was used to color the base). Hold down the corners of the paper with tape (to prevent the paper from shrinking). Next, soak the brush part of the sponge brush in brown liquitex and apply by pressing on.

3．色違いの茶色を同じように重ね塗りする。塗りすぎたらグレーを塗る。

3: Add another layer of a different shade of brown. If you put on too much, you can paint on gray.

4．この石には、ゴールドが入っているので最後にゴールドの缶スプレーを50〜60cm上からサッとかぶせるように塗る。ゴールドを塗りすぎたら茶とグレーを少し足せばよい。

4: The stone contains some gold, so at the end spray some gold at a distance of 50-60 cm from above briskly to cover. If you put on too much gold, you can add a little bit of brown and gray.

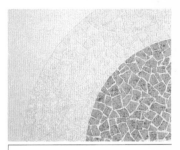

5．紙の裏にスプレーのりをたっぷり塗り、塩ビ板などの板に軽く貼り、ギザギザの帯状に切り、さらに1枚ずつ不揃いに小さく切る。カッターかピンセットで1枚を取り、目地が均等になるように貼る。目地が合わない時は切って使うとよい。

5: Spray on a lot of glue on the reverse side of the paper, and paste lightly onto vinyl chloride board or other board. Cut in jagged strips, then each piece small and irregularly. Remove one piece with the cutter or tweezers, and paste on so that the joints are even. If the joints don't line up, you can snip pieces to make them fit.

6．出来上がり、2種類の石を貼り分けてみた。

6: The finished work. Two different types of stone were pasted on here.

レンガタイルの作り方
コンクリート目地のレンガタイルを作ってみる
対応寸法1/30以上

How to Make Brick Tiles
Making brick tiles with concrete joints   Scale: 1/30 or larger

◆使う物：グレーの塩ビ板、缶スプレー（茶系数本）、アクリルカッター、スチール定規

◆Materials: gray vinyl chloride board, spray paint (several types of brown), acrylic cutter, steel ruler

1．はじめにグレーの塩ビ板に紙ヤスリでキズをつけておき、次に茶色の缶スプレーをサッと50cm位上から乗せるような感じでかけ、乾いたら繰り返し重ね塗りする。かけ過ぎるとテカテカしてレンガらしくなくなるので注意。

1: First use sandpaper on the gray vinyl chloride board to roughen, then spray on a layer of brown paint at a distance of about 50-cm from directly above. When it dries, repeat the application. Avoid getting it too wet with paint, which would make it shiny and not very brick-like.

2: After the paint dries, spray on a different shade of brown in the same way.

2．乾いたら色違いの茶を一度同じようにスプレーする。

３． 最後に黒いツブツブ感を出すためにブラウンをサッとかける。テカリが出てうまくいかなかったらツヤ消しクリヤーを塗るとよい。

3: Finally, to bring out the feel of the tiny black spots, briskly spray on a darker brown. If it becomes too shiny, as a final step you can spray on flat clear paint.

４． 乾いたらアクリルカッターで目地を入れる。横は一直線に入れ、縦は一段ずつ飛ばして引く。横線からはみ出さないように慎重に、コピー定規を使うと便利。(p.19-16参照)

4: When it dries, cut in the joints with the acrylic cutter. First, draw the cutter in a straight line across, then vertically every other line. Be careful not to stray from the horizontal line. Using a copy ruler makes this process easy (See p. 19-16).

５． 出来上がり。

5: The finished work.

６． 階段のレンガは、スチレンペーパーにスチのりで貼ってある。(S＝1/30)

6: The bricks for the stairs are pasted onto styrene paper using styrene glue here (S=1/30).

17 焼過ぎレンガの作り方
How to Make Burnt Brick

◆使う物：スチレンペーパー3mm厚、ボールペン、スチール定規、スコヤ、リキテックス、スポンジ、平筆

◆Materials: 3-mm thick styrene paper, ball-point pen, steel ruler, square, liquitex, sponge, flat brush

１． このような焼過ぎレンガを作ってみる。

1: Let's try making this type of burnt brick.

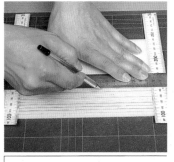

２． スチレンペーパーにボールペンで強めに横目地を書くように掘る。
＊左右の定規はコピー定規。(p.19-16参照)

*2: Use a ball-point pen to press horizontal lines into the styrene paper for joints.
N.B. The rulers on left and right are copy rulers (For more details see p. 19-16).*

３． 縦目地を入れる。

3: Put in the horizontal joints.

４． 写真上のようなくずれた感じを出すには、ボールペンでコーナーなどを押して感じを出す。

4: To bring out the crumbling feel of the brick in the photo at top, use a ball-point pen to press in the corners and other areas.

5. リキテックスの原液を直接スチレンペーパーにつけ、へらで目地に入れる（へらがない場合厚紙でもよい）。目地に入ったら表面のリキテックスはへらでかき取る。

5: Put undiluted liquitex directly onto the styrene paper and use a spatula to put in the joints (If you don't have a spatula, use thick paper). When the joints are in, scrape off the liquitex that is on the surface with the spatula.

6. 目地に入ったリキテックスは乾かないと目地底までやせてくれないので、完全に乾いてから次の作業をするように。（初め表面と目地のリキテックスが同じ高さであるが、乾くとリキテックスが縮み目地底まで下がる）

6: Unless the liquitex in the joints is dry, it will not settle into the bottom of the joint, so it must dry perfectly before the next step is done (At first the liquitex on the surface and in the joints swells up, but it shrinks when it dries and subsides into the bottom of the joint).

7. リキテックスを調合して、スポンジタワシの平たいスポンジの部分で、目地に入り込まないようたたくように塗る。
＊リキテックスは薄めに溶くと目地底に流れてしまうので注意。

7: Mix the liquitex, and using the flat sponge part of the sponge brush, apply by dabbing on so that it does not get in the joints. N.B. If the liquitex is diluted too much, it will run and get into the joints.

8. リキテックスの2、3色を交互に塗り、色を合わせる。

8: Apply two or three colors of liquitex alternately.

10. 出来上がり。左半分が1の写真上のくずれた感じを出している。
＊グレーの目地が残るように塗るのがポイント。

10: The finished work. The left half in photo 1 shows this crumbled texture.
N.B. The key here is to paint so that the gray joints remain intact.

9. 塗料を平筆につけ、数枚2、3色の色を塗る。乾かないうちに塗った塗料をティッシュペーパーで軽く押さえて吸い取り、なじませる。

9: Dip the flat brush into paint and paint several sheets with two or three colors. Before it dries, gently mop up with a tissue.

11. 門柱と塀を作ってみた。目地を入れたスチレンペーパーを4枚、コーナーをトメ（45°）にカットして組み立てた後で、5からの工程で塗装する。アイビーに見立てたものは、木工ボンドをつけた後、2、3mmのグランドフォームをつけてある。

11: Here are a gate post and a wall. Using four sheets of styrene paper with joints, the corners were cut and assembled as miter joints (45 degrees). Then the same method from Step 5 on was used for painting. For structures with climbing ivy, apply wood bond and then 2-3 mm of ground foam.

石積の作り方 石積をスチレンペーパーで作ってみる
How to Make Stone Masonry *Making stone masonry from styrene paper*

◆使う物：スチレンペーパー、ボールペン、木工パテ、スチのり、スチール定規、カッター

◆Materials: styrene paper, ball-point pen, wood putty, styrene glue, steel ruler, cutter

1．この写真を元に石積を作ってみる。

1: Let's try making stone masonry based on this photograph.

2．レンガの作り方の要領で、スチレンペーパーにボールペンで目地を2、3mmの深さに入れる。Rの部分は、サークルカッターで切る。

2: As when making brick, etch joints into styrene paper at a depth of 2-3 mm with a ball-point pen. Cut the curved section using a circle cutter.

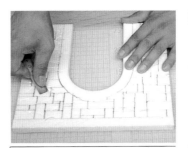

3．石肌の感じを出すためにスチール定規で強く押し、割れ肌の感じを出してみる。

3: To bring out the fissured texture of the stone surface, press down firmly with a steel ruler.

4．出ている石積は、薄いスチレンペーパーを切り出してスチのりで貼る。

4: Cut the masonry work out of thin styrene paper and paste on with styrene glue.

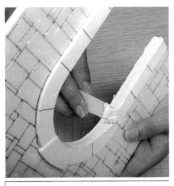

5．貼り合わせた部分は木工パテで埋める。

5: Set in the pasted-on parts using wood putty.

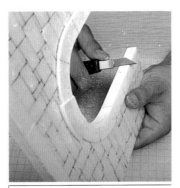

6．木工パテが乾いたら、240番位の紙ヤスリをかけてからカッターで目地をV溝に切り込む。

6: When the wood putty dries, use approximately #240 sandpaper to scratch and then cut in a V-groove using the cutter.

7．全体的にリキテックスのグレーを塗る。
＊石の色もグレーっぽいのでへらでかき取らなくてもよい。

7: Apply gray liquitex to the entire piece.
N.B. Since the stone itself is a gray color, it is not necessary to scrape off with a spatula.

8．色を付ける。初めはスポンジで。塗り方はp.45の7〜9参照。

8: Give it color. First use a sponge. For how to apply, see p. 45, 7-9.

19 敷石の目地に芝を入れる
How to Put Grass in the Joints of Stone Paving

◆使う物：木工ボンド、シーナリパウダー、へら、スポイト、中性洗剤　◆Materials: wood bond, scenery powder, spatula eye dropper, neutral detergent

1．敷石を塗装し、木工ボンドを少量の水で溶き、筆で目地底に塗り込み余分なボンドはゴムべら（厚紙でもよい）で取る。

1: Paint the paving stones, brush wood bond slightly diluted with water into the bottom of the joints and remove the excess bond with a rubber spatula (or thick paper).

2．ボンドは、少し乾かすと目地だけが残る。そこへシーナリパウダーを振りかける。

2: When the bond dries, only the joints are left. Sprinkle scenery powder in the joints.

3．1分位たってからパウダーを取り除いてから吹き飛ばす。

3: Wait about one minute, and after brushing off most of the excess powder, blow off the rest.

4．乾いたら敷石に付いているパウダーはティッシュペーパーで軽くはらう。

4: When it dries, brush any remaining powder off the paving stones lightly with a tissue.

5．パウダーを後から増すには、水で溶いた木工ボンドに、中性洗剤を2、3滴入れ混ぜスポイトに入れ先を細く伸ばす。作り方はp.12-4参照。

5: To add more powder later, dilute wood bond with water, mix in two or three drops of a neutral detergent, draw into an eye dropper and spread with the tip (See p. 12-4).

6．薄めのボンドに中性洗剤が入っているのでパウダーに点でつけるだけでサッとボンドが広がる。＊部分的にボンドをつけたい時には中性洗剤は入れないように。

6: Since there is neutral detergent in the thinned bond, the bond will spread easily by adding just a drop to the powder.
N.B. When you want to put the bond only on a limited area, do not use neutral detergent.

7．もう一度パウダーを振りかけ、すぐに吹き飛ばす。

7: Sprinkle powder once more, then blow the remainder off immediately.

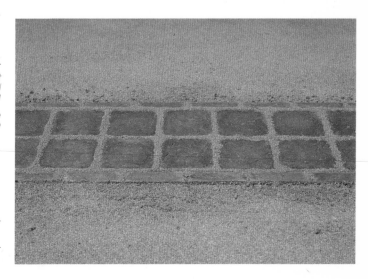

8．出来上がり。

8: The finished model.

崩れたり風化した石の作り方

スチレンペーパーを使い崩れたり
風化した石を作る

How to Make Crumbling or Weathered Stone

Making stone appear in a crumbling
or weathered condition using styrene paper

◆使う物：スチレンペーパー、ラッカーシンナーまたはアク
リダイン、筆

◆Materials: styrene paper, lacquer thinner or acridine
(adhesive for acrylic), brush

1．スチレンペーパーやスタイロ
フォームを使い、石が崩れた感じ
を出すには、あらかじめ余分な部
分をカットしてからシンナーまた
はアクリダインで溶かす。塗り方
はレンガと同じ要領で。

1: To create a crumbling effect
with the stone using styrene paper
or styrofoam, first cut the excess
and dilute with thinner or acridine.
Paint in the same way as with
brick.

2．ツタのからんだ感じにするに
は、水を入れた木工ボンドを細筆
で塗りパウダーをつける。つきが
悪かったら乾かしてからもう一度
重ね塗りする。

2: For the climbing ivy effect, apply
diluted wood bond with a fine
brush and add powder. If it does
not stick well, wait until it dries and
reapply the bond.

3．出来上がり。

3: The finished model.

砂岩の作り方
How to Make Sandstone

◆使う物：塩ビ板、ジェッソ、へら、缶スプレー、スチール定規、アクリルカッター、平筆

◆Materials: vinyl chloride board, gesso, spatula, spray paint, steel ruler, acrylic cutter, flat brush

１．300角の本物の見本。割り肌の感じに注意。

1: This is a 300-mm square sample of the real thing. Notice the cracks on the surface.

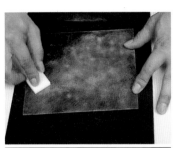

２．塩ビ板やアクリル板などを使う場合、塗料の食いつきをよくするために、紙ヤスリでキズを付ける。

2: When using vinyl chloride board or acrylic board, rub the surface with sandpaper to improve adhesion.

３．ジェッソの原液を平筆で無方向に凹凸を残しながら塗る。ジェッソがない場合はリキテックスの原液でもよい。

3: Apply undiluted gesso with a flat brush in all directions to the indentations and projections. If you do not have gesso, use undiluted liquitex.

４．乾いたら、厚紙で作ったへらで無方向に重ね塗りする。
＊スケールに合わせへらの幅を調整する。

4: When it dries, apply another layer with a spatula made of thick paper in various directions, as shown in the photo to the left.
N.B. Adjust the width of the spatula by aligning with the steel ruler.

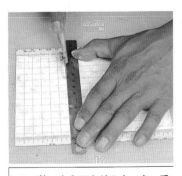

５．乾いたらアクリルカッターでV溝をグリッドに入れる。ここでは９mmピッチになっている。上下にあるコピー定規は、スチール定規を90%に縮小して10mmを9mmに変えてある。（p.19-16参照）

5: When this dries, cut in a V-groove with an acrylic cutter. Here a 9-mm pitch is used. The copy rulers above and below are 90% the size of the steel ruler, changed from 10-mm to 9-mm (See p.19-16).

６．缶スプレーを使って色が合わない場合は、3色位を交互に塗ったり、時には2色一度に塗ると中間色を出せる。
＊2色一度に塗る時は、左右に振りながら40〜50cm離して塗るとよい。

6: When using spray paint, if the color does not match, you can bring out an intermediate color by alternately painting two or three colors or by sometimes painting two colors at once.
N.B. When painting two colors at once, hold at a distance of 40-50 cm and wave the can left and right.

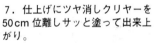

７．仕上げにツヤ消しクリヤーを50cm位離しサッと塗って出来上がり。

7: Use flat clear for the finish, sprayed on briefly from a distance of about 50 cm.

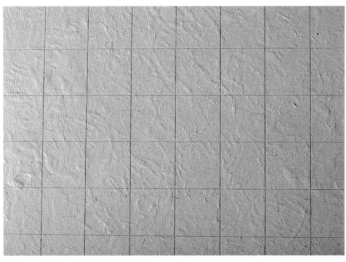

８．色違いの石が混ざっている場合は、アセテートフィルムをグリッドの大きさに切り、ティッシュペーパーにリキテックスを含ませ押しながら塗る。

8: When the stone has mixed colors, cut acetate film to the size of the grid, soak a tissue in liquitex and dab on.

アンティコスタッコの作り方
How to Make Antico Stucco

◆使う物：薄紙、リキテックス、厚紙のへら　　　　　◆Materials: thin paper, liquitex, thick paper spatula

1．アンティコスタッコの実物見本。凹凸はないが、へらで重ねたような跡があることに注目。

1: This is a sample of actual Antico stucco. There are no indentations and projections, but give attention to creating a layered look with the spatula.

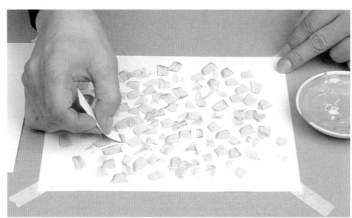

2．リキテックスに水を2、3割入れよく溶いておく。白系の紙に、厚紙をスケールに合わせカットしたへらで、無方向にしごきながら塗料の凹凸を残さないように塗る。ここでは縮小率1/20で作ってある。
＊へらには塗料を少なめにつけた方がよい。紙のコーナーはテープで止める。へらを作る時は先細りにすると丈夫である。

2: Add two or three drops of water to the liquitex and mix well. Use a spatula cut to scale from thick paper to stroke on white-colored paper in various directions to get the paint onto the projections and depressions. A scale of 1/20 was used here.
N.B. It is better to use just a little paint on the spatula. Hold down the corners of the paper with tape. When making the spatula, it is stronger if you make it narrower at the tip.

3．ムラなく無方向に塗り、一度乾かす。
＊乾かす時ドライヤーを使ってもよいが遠くからかけるように。

3: Paint thoroughly in any direction and let dry.
N.B. It is okay to use a dryer, but use it lightly from a distance.

4．茶色が濃かったりムラがあったら白系の茶を同じように重ね塗りする。

4: If the brown color is too dark, or is uneven, you can add a layer of whitish brown on top.

5．出来上がり。模型で壁などに使う場合は裏にスプレーのり（3M-55か77）を吹き付けて使用する。

5: The finished work. If the model is to be used on a wall, use spray glue on the back (3M 55 or 77).

フローリングの作り方
塩ビ板でごくふつうのフローリングを作ってみる

How to Make Flooring
Making ordinary flooring from vinyl chloride board

◆使う物：白の塩ビ板0.5mm厚、アクリルカッター、スチール定規、リキテックス、平筆

◆Materials: white 0.5-mm vinyl chloride board, acrylic cutter, steel ruler, liquitex, flat brush

１．白の塩ビ板を用意し、塗料の食いつきをよくするために紙ヤスリで、溝方向に細かいキズをつける。

1: Prepare the vinyl chloride board and scratch the surface with sandpaper to make the paint adhere better, making fine marks along the grooves.

２．模型の縮小率に従ってアクリルカッターで長い溝を入れる。溝は3mm幅でそろえた（実物は90mm幅でスケール1/30を想定）。溝の深さは浅くすること。深くすると古めかしくなる。コピー定規を使うと便利。(p.19-16参照)

2: Cut in long grooves with the acrylic cutter to the scale of the model. A 3-mm wide groove has been used here (The genuine article has a width of 90-mm. A scale of 1/30 is assumed). The groove is shallow. If it is deep, it becomes old-looking. Using a copy ruler makes this process easy (See p. 19-16).

３．薄めに溶いたリキテックスを塗る。塗り方は溝に平行に流すように何回か往復させ、ムラのないように塗る。
＊塗料が弾いてしまったら中性洗剤を入れる（p.28-26参照）。二度塗りする時は、よく乾かしてから塗るように。

3: To this apply well-diluted liquitex. Paint back and forth spreading parallel to the grooves, so that no part is left uncovered. N.B. If the paint is repelled, add a neutral detergent (See p. 28-26). Before painting a second time, making sure it is thoroughly dry.

４．仕上げの色合いは、初めうすく重ねるごとに本来の色になるので注意。上から一回塗り、二回塗り、三回塗り。重ねればよいというものではないが、重ねると色が変わることを知っていただきたい。また重ね過ぎると色に深みがなくなるので注意。

4: The finish color comes from adding coats upon a thin first layer. From the upper the photos show one coat, two coats and three coats. The key here is not that more coats are better, but that the color changes when you add coats. Also, if you paint too much, the color loses its depth.

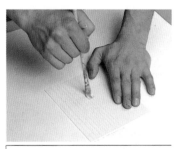

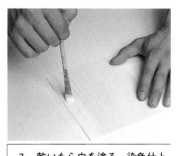

５．ちょっと手を入れて溝の中にフリーハンドでアクリルカッターの溝を入れ、木目風にし、さらに板のつなぎ目も入れた。こうするとリアルなフローリングが出来る。S＝1/20以上の模型に適する。

5: A little care was taken to cut grooves within the grooves freehand with an acrylic cutter to make it look like wood grain, also adding knots. This creates realistic flooring. A 1/20 scale or larger is suitable for the model.

６．塗り方を変えれば白の染色仕上げも出来る。前記と同じ要領で溝を入れる。リキテックスの白に、水を多めに入れ、少し茶色を混ぜてこれも前と同じ要領で塗る。弾く場合は中性洗剤を1、2滴入れるとよい。

6: By changing the method of painting, a white stain finish can be produced. Put in grooves in the same manner as above. Dilute white liquitex with a large amount of water, mix in a little brown color, and paint also in the same way as above. If it is repelled, just add one or two drops of neutral detergent.

７．乾いたら白を塗る。染色仕上げは、下の色に白をかぶせるように塗るのがコツ。
＊乾くと色が変わるので注意。

7: When it dries, paint white. The key to the stain finish is for the white to cover the color below. N.B. The color when dry is different from the color when wet.

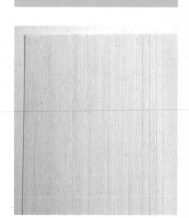

８．出来上がり。

8: The finished work.

本物のヒノキで白木のフローリングを作る

本物のヒノキ材を使って、より本物らしい白木のフローリングを作ってみる　縮小率1/20以上

How to Make Plain Wood with Genuine Hinoki (Japanese Cypress)

Making wood flooring that looks more realistic by using genuine hinoki, at a scale of 1/20 or larger

◆使う物：ヒノキ平材、カッター、スチール定規、木工ボンド、紙ヤスリ、クリヤー

◆Materials: flat boards of hinoki, cutter, steel ruler, wood bond, sandpaper, clear paint

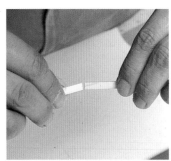

１．市販のヒノキの平らな細長い板（1mm厚）を用意する。バルサでもよいが重量感がないので、より本物らしく見せたい時はヒノキの方がよい。これにカッターで長、中、短の3種類の切れ目を入れる。

1: Prepare a long, flat board of hinoki that is sold in stores (1-mm thick). Balsa wood is also okay, but it does not look heavy enough. When you want to create a more realistic feel, hinoki is better. With a cutter, insert three lengths of fold lines: long, medium and short.

２．切れ目を入れたら、そこから折る。もし切り口にササクレができたらヤスリをかけて平らにする。

2: After inserting the lines, fold along them. If a fine split develops on the end, smooth flat with a file.

３．ミニ丸鋸を使うと便利。上の機械は特製スライステーブルをつけ、より正確に、より安全に切ることができる。

3: A small circular saw makes this process easy. Use a small circular saw blade on a table saw to cut more accurately and more safely.

４．3種類の長さのヒノキ材を台紙（コピー用紙など）に貼る。貼り方は一枚ずつ板の端にボンドを付けて貼る。

4: Paste the three types of hinoki (long, medium and short) onto mounting paper (copy paper, e.g.). Put bond on the edges of each board and paste onto the mount.

５．板を重ね、はみ出たボンドはティッシュペーパーでよくふき取る。乾かす場合このままでは反ってしまうので上から重しを乗せて乾かす。

5: Stack the boards and wipe away any excess bond that is squeezed out. The boards will warp if left this way, so place a weight on top and then let dry.

６．乾いたら木工用紙ヤスリをかける。はじめは粗めのもので凹凸をなくしてから目の細かいものでスベスベにしていく。紙ヤスリは継ぎ目に沿ってかける。

6: When they dry, rub with sandpaper for use with wood. First use coarse sandpaper to eliminate indentations and projections, then use fine sandpaper to make it smooth. Rub with the grain.

７．床の大きさに切ってツヤ出しクリヤーの缶スプレーを満遍なく塗る。一度乾かし、軽くヤスリがけしてもう一度塗る。

7: Cut to the size of the floor, and spray thoroughly with glossy clear spray paint. Let it dry, lightly rub with sandpaper again and paint once more.

８．出来上がり。これは床材だけでなく、集成材のテーブルの甲板としても使える。

8: The finished product. This is not only flooring material. It can also be used as the top for a plywood table.

本物のヒノキで白の染色仕上げを作る

リキテックスをタオルで拭き取り
染色仕上げを作る

How to Make a White Stain Finish with Genuine Hinoki (Japanese Cypress)

Making a stain finish by wiping off liquitex with a towel

◆使う物：リキテックス、平筆、タオル、クリヤー　　　　◆Materials: liquitex, flat brush, towel, clear spray paint

１．ヒノキのフローリングに、継ぎ目方向に筆を流すようにリキテックスの白を塗る。弾くようであれば中性洗剤を入れる。
＊木は水を含むと反ってしまうのですばやく作業するのがコツ。

1: Paint the hinoki flooring with white liquitex. Spread with the grain using a brush. If it gets repelled, add neutral detergent. N.B. If the wood absorbs water it will warp, so paint as quickly as possible.

２．乾かないうちに継ぎ目方向にタオルで拭き取る。

2: Before it dries, use a towel to wipe off the paint with the grain.

３．出来上がり。クリヤーを塗ればツヤが出る。ここでは白を塗ったがグレーも同じ要領で。

3: The finished work. If you spray with clear paint it will bring out the luster. White was used here, but gray may be used instead.

26

モザイクパーケットの作り方

モザイクパーケットの作り方
柾目を互い違いにして

How to Make a Mosaic Packet

Employ straight grain alternately

◆使う物：壁紙材、カッター、スチール定規、スプレーのり、台紙、クリヤー　　　　◆Materials: wallpaper, cutter, steel ruler, spray glue, mounting paper, clear spray paint

１．高級壁紙材「サンフット」北三（株）などの柾目を使い、裏にスプレーのりをかけて下敷きに貼る。それをカッターでマス目に切る。今回は10mm角に切る。コピー定規を使うと便利。サンフットはスギ柾目使用。

1: Using straight-grain high-quality wallpaper such as "Sunfoot" from HOXAN, spray glue on the back and paste onto substrate. Cut into squares with the cutter. This time the squares were cut in 10-mm pieces. Using a copy ruler makes this process easy (See p. 19-16). Sunfoot uses straight-grained cedar.

２．台紙となる紙（ケント紙）と壁紙の両方にスプレーのりをかけると丈夫に貼れる。

2: Next, also spray glue on the mounting paper (kent paper). Spray on both of the surfaces to be pasted together, except when the wallpaper has an adhesive on the back. Spray glue 3M 55 was used here.

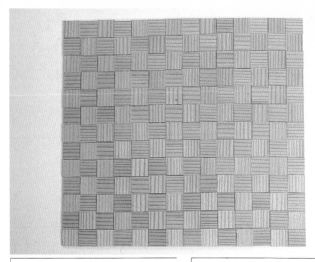

3．柾目が互い違いになるように
一枚一枚台紙に貼っていく。
＊色を変える場合は１のマスに切
る前にリキテックスで塗り、拭き
取るかマーカーで色を塗っておく。

3: Paste one by one onto the mounting paper so that the straight grain alternates.
N.B. If you want to change the color, before cutting into squares, either paint with liquitex and wipe off, or color with a marker.

4．全部貼り終わったらよく乾か
しクリヤーの缶スプレーを満遍な
くかけツヤを出す。こうすると本
物の床らしく見える。

4: After pasting all of the squares on, let it dry completely and then spray on clear paint thoroughly to bring out the luster. When you do this it comes to resemble genuine flooring.

5．出来上がり。貼り合わせ部分
が目立つようであれば色に合わせ
た濃いめのリキテックスをへらで
目地に埋め、ティッシュペーパー
でよくふき取るとよい。

5: The finished work. If the pasted-on parts stand out, put a slightly darker color of liquitex into the joints and wipe off well with a tissue.

6．家具店の模型。壁の赤と青の
ストライプはインスタントレタリ
ング（クロマテック）で作り貼って
ある。床はABS板にアクリルカッ
ターで直線にV溝を入れてから、
フリーハンドで板目を入れ、リキ
テックスで塗ってある。什器もABS
板で作った。
Design：白水社、S＝1/20

6: Design: Hakusuisha Publishing Company Ltd.　Scale: 1/20
A model for a bedding store. The red and blue stripes on the wall are made by pasting on Inletter (Chromatech) line tape. The floor is made of ABS board with V-grooves cut in straight lines with a cutter and a cross grain put in freehand and painted with liquitex. The cabinet is made of ABS board.

27

椅子の作り方
黒い布張りの椅子　モデル／カッシーナLima　S=1/30

How to Make a Chair
Chair with a black cloth seat. Model/Catthina Lima S=1/30

◆使う物：1mm角の真鍮棒、ニッパ、三角ヤスリ、ハンダゴテ、ステンレス用フラックス、ABS板1mm厚、紙ヤスリ、缶スプレー、両面テープ

◆Materials: 1-mm square brass rod, nipper, triangular file, soldering iron, flux for stainless steel, 1-mm thick ABS board, sandpaper, spray paint, both-sided tape

１．椅子の脚になる真鍮棒（1mm角）を用意して、ニッパで適当な長さにカットする。次にこの棒で前脚と座面を支える台輪（貫）を作る。直角に折り曲げるために、その部分に三角ヤスリをかけて45度の切り口を入れる。

1: Prepare brass rod (1-mm square) for the chair legs. Cut to a suitable length with the nipper. Next, make the base (stretcher) that supports the front legs and seat. To be able to bend this at a right angle, use a metal file to put in a edge at a 45-degree angle at that location.

２．直角に折り曲げる。

2: Bend at a right angle.

３．折り曲げたら、図面に当て長さを合わせカッターで印をつけてからニッパで切り、切り口をヤスリがけしておく。

3: Once it is bent, put a mark at the appropriate length by placing against the drawing with the cutter, then cut with the nipper, and file down the edge.

４．後脚の部分も図面に当ててちょうどいい長さにニッパでカットする。

4: Measure the area for the rear legs by placing against the drawing, and cut to the proper length with the nipper.

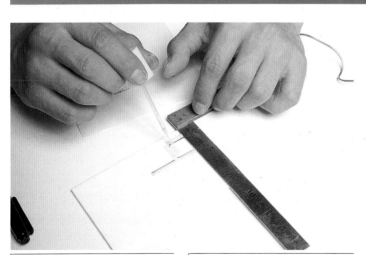

５．この2本の真鍮棒をハンダ付けする前に、これらを固定するハンダ付け用の型を作る。台（アクリル板）に薄く細いアクリル棒かABS板を切ったものを適当な長さに切って貼る。図面の寸法通りになるように、貼る位置に前もって線を引いておく。

5: You are going to solder the two brass rods together, but first you must fix them in position. Cut a long, thin acrylic rod or ABS board to the proper length and paste to the mount (acrylic board). Draw a line in the proper position ahead of time so that the dimensions match the drawings.

６．型ができたら真鍮棒をはめ込んでハンダ付けする。ステンレス用の「フラックス」を塗るとハンダ付けしやすい。ハンダ付けするのは手で折り曲げた部分と、後脚と座面が接する部分。

6: When the shape is held, fit in the brass rod and solder on. Soldering is easier if you apply "flux" for stainless steel. The part to be soldered is where the curved part you hold with your hand contacts the rear legs and seat.

７．次に背板と座面になるABS板1mm厚を用意し、まず背の幅に合わせ細長く持ちやすいようにカットする。このモデルの背板は微妙に曲がっているのでABS板の先をハンダゴテに近づけて加熱し、柔らかくする。

7: Next, prepare 1-mm thick ABS board for the backboard and seat. First, measure the width and cut long and thin so that it is easy to hold. The backboard on this chair curves ever so slightly. Move the soldering iron close to the edge of the ABS board, and heat it up to soften it.

8．柔らかくなったらABS板の先を丸い筒状のものに押し当てて丸みをつける。

8: Press the softened edge of ABS board against a round pipe to make it round.

9．固まったら表面に紙ヤスリをかけ形をきれいにする。

9: When it hardens, use sandpaper to smooth out the shape.

10．それをちょうどいい長さにカットすれば背板が出来上がる。座面も幅に合わせカットし同様に作る。

10: If you were able to cut to just the right length, then the backboard is done. Align the width of the seat, cut and make in the same way.

11．塗装は、脚と背、座板の部分は質感が違うので別々にスプレーする。脚は両面テープで貼る。

11: Painting is done next, but since the feel of the material is different for the legs, back and seat, they must be sprayed separately. Put legs onto both-sided tape.

12．立てたら黒の缶スプレーを塗る。

12: Stand the chair and spray it with black paint.

13．背と座もスプレーする。布張りの感じを出したいので、何回かに分けてスプレーする。初めは満遍なく塗り、次に50cm位離して霧をかぶせるような感じでスプレーする。こうするとザラザラになり布の感じが出せる。

13: Spray the back and seat as well. Since you want to elicit the feel of cloth, spray in several steps. The first few times spray very lightly and briskly so that it does not shine. Next, mist on from a distance of about 50-cm. This creates the coarse feel of cloth.

14．乾いたら、椅子の脚にスチのりで接着する。この時接着しやすくするために11の固定の時に脚の幅を合わせておくと楽である。

14: When it dries, attach the chair legs with styrene glue. To make this process easier, align the width when fixing the position in Step 11.

15．十分時間をかけてスチのりが固まったら、はずして出来上がり。スチのりは少しゆるめにして使うとよい。（p.12-5参照）

15: Allow plenty of time for the styrene glue to harden, remove and the model is done.

16．ミニカッティングソーを使うと便利。カットする時テープで真鍮棒を数本まとめて切れば速く切れ、長さもそろう。45°も切ることができる。プロクソン社製。

16: Using a small cutting saw makes it easier to build this model. When cutting, put tape on several brass rods and cut them all together. This saves time and unifies the lengths. You are also able to cut at a 45-degree angle (brand: PROXXON).

ハイスツールを作る
How to Make a High Stool

◆使う物：真鍮棒、角材、ニッパ、ペンチ、ハンダ、ハンダゴテ、フラックス、鉄ヤスリ、缶スプレー

◆Materials: brass rod, square rod, nipper, pinch, cutting pliers, solder, soldering iron, flux, steel file, spray paint

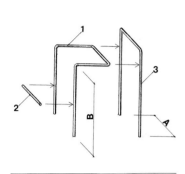

1．パーツ図。

1: Drawing of part.

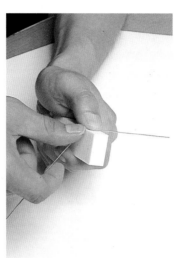

２．脚になる真鍮の丸棒（太さ0.7mm）を用意する。2本の前脚と座枠を1本の棒を折り曲げて作る。図1。この時は角材（アクリル板、ABS板、木材）を型として使う。角材は一辺を椅子の幅Aに、もう一辺を前脚の長さBに合わせて作る。このゲージがあればいくつでも同じものが作れる。

2: Prepare round brass rod (0.7-mm) for the legs. Make the two front legs and seat out of one bent rod (Drawing 1). Use square pieces (acrylic or ABS board, wood) for the form. Align the pieces first for the chair width (A) and a second time for the length of the front legs (B) before building. Once you have this gauge, you can make as many of the same piece as you wish.

３．まず真鍮棒を角材に当て角のところで左右にコの字形に折る。角材をまたぐような形になる。

3: First, place the brass rod against the square piece and bend the corners to form a squared "U" shape, in effect straddling the square piece.

４．それを一度ゲージからはずしてコの字形の角の部分をペンチで直角に整える。

4: Remove from the gauge at this point and use a cutting pliers to sharpen the corner right angles.

５．コの字形につながったところから座面の長さを合わせて、角材の角に当てて直角に折る。折った下半分が前脚になる。

5: Align the length of the seat from the point that connects to the "U" shape, press against the corner of the square piece and bend to a right angle. The bent lower part becomes the front legs.

６．前脚となる真鍮棒は角材にピッタリ付ける。前脚の長さBに合わせて、真鍮棒のはみ出た部分をニッパでカットする。

6: Fit the brass rods that will be the front legs tightly against the square piece. Align the length of the front legs with B, and cut the part of the brass rod that sticks out with the nipper.

７．この2本の前脚の間に足掛け2をハンダ付けする。27の項目でやったように型を作ってそこにはめ込んで付ける。

7: Solder on the footrests (2) between the two front legs. Hold the position firm as shown on the previous page and fit together.

８．次に背もたれの枠と後脚になる部分3を作る。これも1本の真鍮棒を角材に当ててコの字形に曲げる。これを角材の型にはめてある脚1に合わせ、動かないようテープで止め3との接点をハンダ付けする。

8: Next, make the frame for the flame and the part that will become the rear legs. This is also made from one brass rod bent into a squared "U" by laying against a square piece. Line this up with the legs (1) fit to the shape of the square piece, hold in place with cellophane tape and solder where it contacts (3).

９．ハンダ付けした部分の表面に鉄ヤスリをかける。

9: File the surface of the soldered part with a metal file.

10．さらに紙ヤスリをかけて表面をきれいにする。その後、中性洗剤を入れたお湯で洗う。

10: Then sand the surface with sandpaper to make it smooth. Later rinse with hot water that has neutral detergent in it.

11．ABS板1mm厚で座面を作り、スチのりで接着し黒の缶スプレーを満遍なくかける。座の色が違う場合は別々に塗る。

11: Make the seat from 1-mm thick ABS board and attach with styrene glue. Then spray thoroughly with black spray paint. If the seat part is a different color, paint it separately.

12．出来上がり。右は1.5mm角の真鍮棒で作ってある。作り方は27とここでやった作り方のミックスで作れる。

12: The finished model. On the right is a stool made from 1.5-mm square brass rod. It was made with a mixture of this technique and the one described on the previous pages.

塩ビ板で作る簡単な椅子とテーブル
塩ビ板を折るだけで作れる椅子とポンチで作るテーブル

Making a Simple Table and Chair from Vinyl Chloride Board
A chair can be made simply by folding vinyl chloride board and a table with a hole puncher

◆使う物：塩ビ板0.5mm、カッター、スチール定規、ポンチ、カナヅチ、プラスチック棒、瞬間接着剤　◆Materials: 0.5-mm vinyl chloride board, cutter, hole puncher, hammer, plastic rod, instant bond

1．椅子の幅に合わせて塩ビ板に細長く切れ目を入れた後、縦方向に数カ所カッターで折り目を入れる。折り目は背と座の境目（裏面）、座と前脚の境目、前脚と下で支える脚の境目（表面）、計3カ所に入れる。

1: Align the vinyl chloride board with the chair width and put in a long, thin cut line. Also put in vertical fold lines in three places. One should be at the border of the back and the seat (cut on the reverse side), the second at the border of the seat and the front legs, and the third at the border of the front legs and the legs that support below.

2．椅子の幅で入れた切れ目に合わせ折って切り離す。今度は一つ一つゆっくり折って曲げる。

2: Bend along the cut lines along the width of the chair and cut free. Next, fold one by one.

3．形を整えたら出来上がり。小さなインテリア模型の中に置いて家具のレイアウトを見たい時などは、この程度の椅子でも十分役に立つ。

3: After you firm up the shape the model is complete. This simple of model of a chair is very helpful for placing in a small interior model when, for example, you just want to see the layout.

4．丸テーブルを簡単に作ってみる。塩ビ板0.5mmをポンチを使って天板と台座を抜く。プラスチック棒を切り、瞬間接着剤で止める。

4: Let's try making a simple round table. Use a hole puncher on 0.5-mm vinyl chloride board to cut out a hole in the table top and base. Cut a plastic rod, insert and fix in place with instant bond.

5．出来上がり。脚は接着前に黒の缶スプレーで塗ってある。あるいは、脚を付けてから全体を缶スプレーで塗ってもよい。

5: The finished model. Before attaching legs, paint with black spray paint. It is also okay to put legs on and then spray the entire piece.

30 白木の椅子の作り方
How to Make a Plain Wood Chair

◆使う物：ABS板2mm厚、スチール定規、カッター、糸のこ、紙ヤスリ（ハレパネに貼った物）、アクリダイン、缶スプレー、ツヤ消しクリヤー、クリヤー

◆Materials: ABS board 2-mm thick, steel ruler, cutter, fret saw, sandpaper (pasted onto adhesive styrene board), acridine, liquitex, flat clear and glossy clear spray paint

１．これから作る椅子の実物写真。
IDÉE IPC-19 WOOD CHAIR

1: A picture of the chair you are going to make. IDÉE IPC-19 Wood Chair

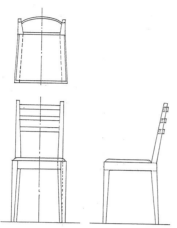

２．写真から図面をおこす。

2: Create drawings from the photograph.

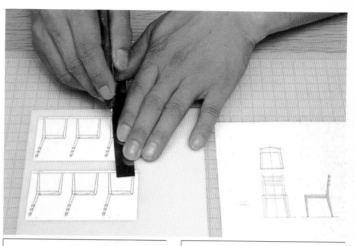

３．側面図をコピーしスプレーのり（3M-55）を軽く吹きかけABS板2mmに貼る。次にカッターで図面の上から線に合わせ切れ目を入れる。

3: Copy the side-view drawing, spray lightly with spray glue (3M 55) and paste onto 2-mm ABS board. Then, along the lines of the drawing, put in cut lines from the top with a cutter.

４．コピー用紙をはがし、鉛筆の粉をティッシュペーパーでこするとカッターのラインが見えやすくなる。

4: Peel off the copy paper, rub on pencil lead with a tissue to make the lines more visible.

５．線に合わせ糸のこで切り出す。

5: Cut along the lines with a fret saw.

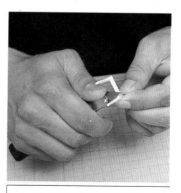

６．糸のこの切り残し、特にコーナーはカッターで切り線に合わせる。

6: The parts left uncut by the fret saw, particularly the corners, need to be cut with the cutter along the lines.

７．ハレパネに貼った紙ヤスリ（240番）を幅に合わせカットし線のところまでヤスリがけする。

7: Line up sandpaper (#240) pasted onto adhesive styrene paper along the width, cut and sand up to the lines.

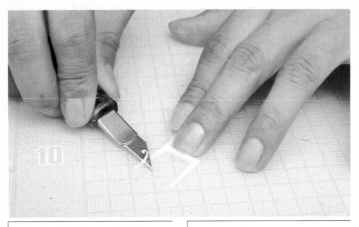

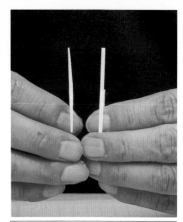

8．脚の先と背の先を細くする。カッターで少しずつカットして先細りにしていく。切り過ぎたら切った破片をアクリダインで貼り合わせ、乾いたら直る。

8: Taper the ends of the legs and back. Cut little by little with the cutter to make the end narrow. If you cut too much, paste on acridine and fix it when it dries.

9．カット面に紙ヤスリをかけ平らにする。

9: Make the cut surface flat by sanding with sandpaper.

10．左のように先細りにヤスリがけする。

10: Sand to a tapered end as shown to the left.

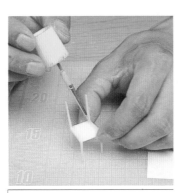

11．座の受けを作る。左右の脚を固定する材料にもなる。ABS板 2mm を使い脚の内側に切れ目を入れる。

11: Make the seat support. It will also serve as material to fix the left and right legs in place. Use 2-mm ABS board and put a cut line on the inside of the legs.

12．切れ目に沿って折り、切り離す。

12: Bend along the cut lines, cut and remove.

13．ヤスリがけしてから左右の脚と接着する。

13: After sanding, attach to the left and right legs.

14．背板を切り出す。1mmのABS板を使い0.5mm幅でカットする。初め軽くカッターで切れ目を入れてから一挙に切り出す。

14: Cut out the backboard. Use 1-mm ABS board and cut with a cutter 0.5-mm wide. First put in a cut line lightly with the cutter and then cut away all at once.

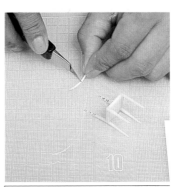

15．切り口の両面をヤスリがけしてから、角材の端を持ち丸い棒に当て、指で押さえながら引くと曲げられる。それ以上小さいRにならない場合は、小さい丸棒に代えればよい。

15: Use sandpaper to smooth both of the cut ends. Hold the end of the square piece, place against a round rod and while holding with a finger, bend by pulling it. Repeat this process. When the curved section does not get any smaller, change to a small rod.

16．背板を取り付ける位置に印をつける。背板を幅に合わせカッターで押すように切る。

16: Place a mark where the backboard is to be attached. Align the width of the backboard and cut by pressing with the cutter.

17．背板をアクリダインで接着する。

17: Attach the backboard using acridine.

18. 座面を作る。座は1mmのABS板を使い、座の受けと同じ要領で切り出し、端をヤスリがけして丸みをつける。座の色を変える場合は本体と接着しないように。

18: Make the seat. Use 1-mm ABS board, cut away in the same manner as with the seat support, sand down the ends with sandpaper and round them off. If you want to change the color of the seat, do not attach to the frame.

19. 左が出来上がり。右は1mmのABS板で作ったS=1/30の椅子とテーブル。

19: On the left is the finished model. On the right is a table and chair made of 1-mm ABS board at a scale of 1/30.

20. 下地塗装する。木部を両面テープで固定し、木の色に近い色を塗る。

20: Paint the substrate. Fix the wood in place using both-sided tape, and paint with a color that is close to the wood color.

21. 下地塗装が乾いたらリキテックスで色を出し、筆塗りする。テーブルに縁材がある場合は、マスキングテープで縁をマスキングし中から塗るとよい。

21: When the substrate paint dries, bring out the color with liquitex and paint with a brush. If the table has a rim, cover the rim with masking tape and paint from the middle.

22. 乾いたらマスキングテープを取り、筆で周りを塗る。この時はみ出てしまったらすぐにティッシュペーパーで拭き取ればまた塗ることができる。

22: When it dries, remove the masking tape and paint the rim with a brush. If any paint overflows, immediately wipe off with a tissue and paint again.

23. 椅子とテーブルにクリヤーを塗ってツヤを出す。

23: Apply clear paint to bring out the luster of the chair and table.3

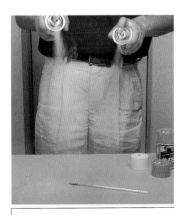

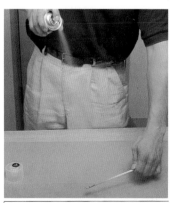

24. 座面を塗る。2、3色の缶スプレーを使い色を合わせる。このように2本いっぺんに塗ると混ざりやすく中間色が出しやすい。

24: Paint the seat. Use two or three colors of spray paint to adjust the color. Painting two colors at once makes the colors blend easily to help bring out an intermediate tone.

25. 仕上げにツヤ消しクリヤーを50cm位離し、塗料を乗せるように塗ると布の質感が出る。

25: For the finish, spray on flat clear paint at a distance of approximately 50-cm as if laying on, to bring out the feel of cloth.

26. 出来上がり。座の色はサーモンピンクに変えてある。

26: The finished model. Here, the color of the seat was changed to salmon pink.

31

ヨーロッパ調の椅子を作る
Making a European-style Chair

◆使う物：ABS板2mm厚、糸のこ、スチール定規、アクリダイン、ファンド、ベビーパウダー、缶スプレー、リキテックス、面相筆、クリヤー

◆Materials: 2-mm thick ABS board, fret saw, steel ruler, acridine, foundation, baby powder, spray paint, liquitex, fine brush, clear paint

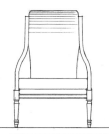

１．これから作る椅子の実物写真。

1: A picture of the chair we are going to make.

２．写真から図面をおこす。

2: Create drawings from the picture.

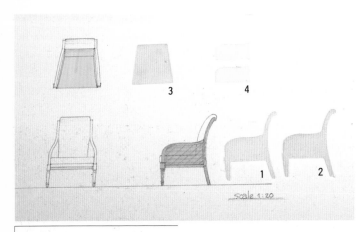

scale 1:20

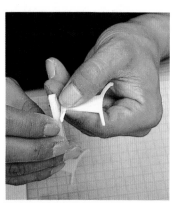

３．各パーツ。1と2が脚と背の一体形、3座の受け材、4側面の布地材。

3: The various parts. The legs and back of 1 and 2 are a single unit. 3 is the seat support material and 4 a side view of the cloth substrate.

４．白木の椅子の作り方p.59の3〜9までと同じ要領で1と2の材を切り出し、上の図の黒い部分をカッターでV溝に4面切り、窪みをつける。

4: Using the same steps you used to make a plain wood chair (p. 59, 3-9), cut free 2-mm-thick board, cut a V-groove on four sides marked by the red part in the drawing above to make a well.

５．V溝に紙ヤスリをかける。脚の先も丸みをつける。

5: Sand the V-groove with a corner of sandpaper. Round off the bottom of the legs.

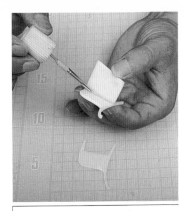

6．座の受けを取り付ける。

6: Attach the seat support.

7．側面の布地材4を切り出す。ここでは0.5mmのABS板を使っているが、塩ビ板でもよい。コーナーは丸みをつけておく。

7: Cut out four pieces of cloth for the sides. Here, 0.5-mm ABS board was used, but vinyl chloride board is also okay. Round the corners.

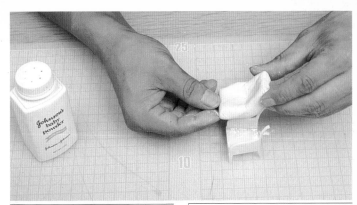

8．座面を作る。ファンド（細密造形用粘土）をあらかじめ座の形にしてから底と側面にベビーパウダーをつけておく。
＊ベビーパウダーをつけないと後で取れなくなるので注意。

8: Make the seat. Shape the foundation (modeling clay for making delicate objects) into the seat ahead of time, then apply baby powder to the bottom and the sides.
N.B. If you don't use baby powder, it will become impossible to remove later.

9．型に押し込みスチール定規に水をつけ座の奥から座の丸みをつけながら形を整える。

9: Press clay into a mold, and adjust the shape with a steel ruler dipped in water from the back end of the seat while rounding the seat.

10．ニッパなどで余分なファンドは切る。

10: Cut off the excess clay using a nipper or other tool.

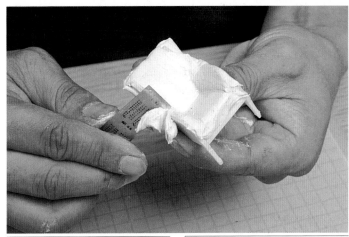

11．水をつけた定規で背からひじ掛けの部分に沿ってそぎ落とす。

11: With a steel ruler dipped in water, shave from the back to the armrest.

12．背も同じように余分なファンドは切り取り、指で丸みをつけこのまま1日乾かす。

12: Cut away excess clay in the same way for the back, round with your fingers, and let dry for one day.

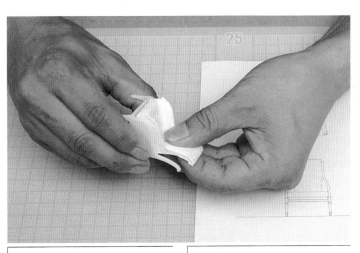

13．ファンドが乾いたら無理せずゆっくり型から取り出す。底の部分が乾いてなかったら底を上にしてさらに乾かす。網のような風通しのよいものの上に置き乾かすとよい。

13: When the foundation clay dries, gently remove from the mold. If the bottom part is not dry, turn it over and let it dry. Place it on a screen or other material that lets the air pass through.

14．完全に乾いたらカッターで形を整える。

14: When it is completely dry, trim with a cutter.

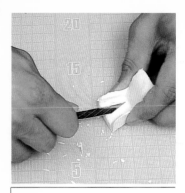

15. コーナーはカッターで切る。

15: Cut the corners with a cutter.

16. カッターの届かない部分は平刃で切り、コーナーを整える。

16: Where the cutter cannot reach, cut with a flat blade and trim the corners.

17. 紙ヤスリをハレパネに貼ったものを各部分に合わせカットしたもので細部までヤスリがけする。

17: Sand. Align each part, cut and sand down the narrow areas with sandpaper (pasted onto adhesive styrene paper).

18. このようにヤスリをかけ丸みをつける。隙間やキズがあったら木工パテで補修する。

18: Sand in this way to round it.

19. 各パーツに色を塗る。左はブラウンの缶スプレーを塗り乾いたらクリヤーを塗る。右は布地のパーツ4も含めベースの色を缶スプレーで塗っておく。

19: Paint the various parts to color them. On the left a brown spray paint was used and then clear once the brown had dried. On the right, a base color was sprayed on, including the cloth part (4).

20. 布の模様をリキテックスで描く。

20: Draw on the cloth pattern with liquitex.

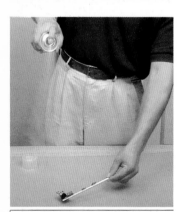

21. 模様が乾いたらツヤ消しクリヤーを50cm位離してかぶせるように塗り、ツヤを消し布の感じを出す。

21: When the pattern dries, spray on flat gray from a distance of about 50-cm just to cover. This will dull the gloss and create the feel of cloth.

22. スチのりでパーツを接着する。

22: Attach parts with styrene glue.

23. 出来上がり。

23: The finished model.

32

ネコ脚の椅子を作る
How to Make a Chair with Carved Legs

◆使う物：ABS板3mm、糸のこ、カッター、ペンチ、ハンダゴテ、アクリダイン、ポリパテ、スチレンペーパー、リキテックス、缶スプレー

◆Materials: 3-mm thick ABS board, fret saw, cutter, cutting pliers, soldering iron, acridine, polyester putty, styrene paper, liquitex, spray paint

1．これから作る椅子の実物写真。

1: A picture of the chair we are going to make.

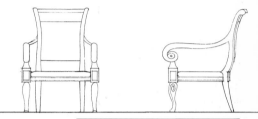

2．写真を元に図面をおこす。

2: Create drawings from the picture.

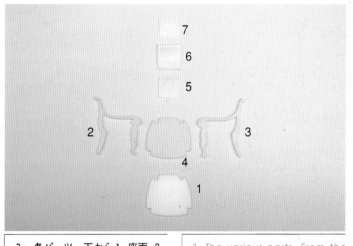

3．各パーツ。下から 1.座面、2.
3.脚と背の一体形、4.座の受け、
5.背の前の布地材、6.背の木部、
7.背の後ろの布地材。

3: The various parts. From the bottom: 1. seat; 2 and 3. single unit of legs and back; 4. seat support; 5. material for the front part of the back; 6. wood part of the back; 7. material for the rear part of the back

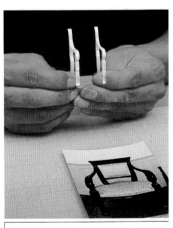

4．まずABS板 3mm を糸のこで切り抜く。作り方は p.59の3〜9と同じ要領で、脚のくぼみは右のようにカッターで4面V溝にカットし、紙ヤスリをかける。肘掛けも細くヤスリがけする。

4: First cut out from 3-mm ABS board using a fret saw. Using the same method as on p. 59, 3-9, cut V-grooves on four sides for the leg wells as shown on the right, and sand with sandpaper. Also make the armrest with fine sanding.

5．肘掛けの曲がりは、ハンダゴテをスタンドに置き、1cm位離して曲げる部分を熱しゆっくり曲げる。

5: For the curve of the armrest, place the soldering iron in a stand, slowly heat the area, and bend.

6．このように左右同じ曲がりになるように。

6: Bend both left and right in the same manner.

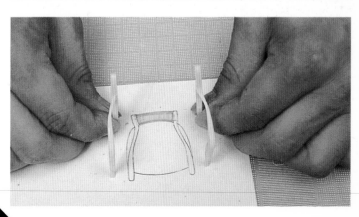

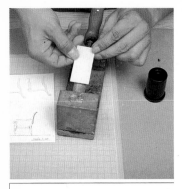

7．背の木部（6）を作る。ハンダゴテの上に1、2cm離し大きめに切った1mmのABS板をのせる。

7: Make the wood part (6) of the back. Place a large section of 1-mm ABS board 1-2 cm away from the tip of the soldering iron.

8．十分に柔らかくなったABS板を背の曲がりに合った丸棒に押しつける。熱いので軍手をするとよい。

8: When the ABS board has become soft enough, press against a round rod that matches the curve of the back. Wear cotton gloves because the board is hot.

9．もう一度熱しペンチで先をはさみ、折り曲げる。2方向に曲げることにより、3次曲面が出来る。次に大きさに合わせカットし紙ヤスリで形を整える。

9: Heat once more and bend the edges with cutting pliers. By bending in two directions you can create a 3D curve. Next, cut to the right size, and trim the shape with sandpaper.

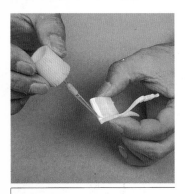

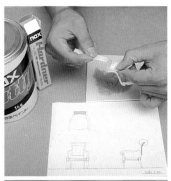

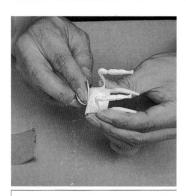

10．背材（6）をアクリダインで取り付ける。背の前と後ろの布地材（5、7）も同じようにABS板か塩ビ板の0.5mmで背材（6）に合わせ曲げる。

10: Remove the back material (6) using acridine. Align and bend the material for the front and rear parts of the back (5, 7) in the same way with ABS board or vinyl chloride board.

11．接着部分と背の曲がりの部分にポリパテを盛っておく。

11: Hold together the part to attach and the back curve with polyester putty.

12．紙ヤスリを指に巻き、曲面部分から接着部分をヤスリがけする。

12: Wrap sandpaper around your finger and sand from the curved part to the attached part.

13．座の受け（4）を作る。3mmのABS板に図面を貼り、カッターで切れ目を入れる。

13: Make the chair support (4). Paste on 3-mm ABS board and put in a cut line with a cutter.

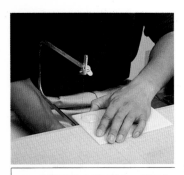

14．鉛筆の粉を擦り込み、線に合わせ糸のこで切り出す。切り口は紙ヤスリをかける。

14: Rub on pencil lead and cut out with a fret saw along the line. Sand down the edges with sandpaper.

15．座面（1）を作る。スチレンペーパー3mmに座の受け（4）をのせ、マジックで書く。
＊書いた面が裏になるので受けと座の接着面を間違えないように。

15: Make the seat (1). Place the seat support (4) onto 3-mm styrene paper and draw with a magic marker.
N.B. The surface drawn on will become the back, so do not confuse the adhesive side of the support and seat.

16．線に合わせ少し大きめにカットする。後でヤスリ型を作るので切り過ぎないように。

16: Cut along the lines leaving a little extra room. Later you can file down to the proper shape.

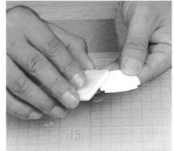

17. 裏返してカッターで端をそぐ
ようにカットし、丸みを出す。

17: Turn over, and cut with the cutter along the edge to round off.

18. 紙ヤスリをかけ、さらに丸み
を出す。

18: Round with sandpaper.

19. 受け材（4）に合っているか確
認する。

19: Confirm that it lines up with the support material (4) and that it was not filed down too much or does not stick out too much.

20. 布地を塗る。座（1）と背の布
地（5、7）をプラモデル用缶スプ
レーで色に合わせ塗り、面相筆で
模様を描く。
＊座がスチレンペーパーなのでラ
ッカースプレーを使うと溶けてし
まうので注意。

20: Paint the cloth. Spray the seat (1) and back cloth (5,7) with colored paint for plastic models and draw on the pattern with a fine brush.
N.B. The seat is made of styrene paper and will melt if a lacquer spray is used.

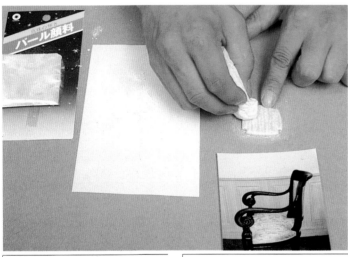

21. 写真の布地はパールに光る布
なのでこの模型でもパール顔料を
ティッシュペーパーでこすりつけ
光らせる。定着剤（パステルなど
の保護用スプレー）を塗り、パー
ル顔料をコーティングする。
パール顔料：（株）クラチ、定着材：
（株）バニーコーポレーション使用

21: The cloth in the photo shines like pearl, so a pearl pigment must be rubbed on with a tissue to make it shine. Use a fixative (spray for protecting pastels, etc.) to coat the pearl pigment.

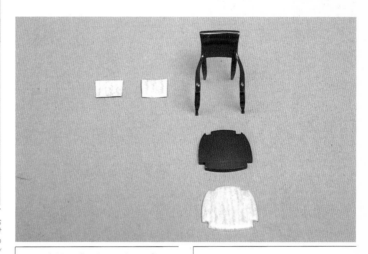

22. 木部はブラウンの缶スプレー
を塗る。座の受け（4）に取り付け
てから組み立てる。接着剤はスチ
のりで。

22: Paint the wood part with brown spray paint. If you attach the seat support (4) first, the seat (1) will not fit in, so after attaching the support material (4), "assemble" using styrene glue as the adhesive.

革張りの椅子を作る
Making a Leather Upholstery Chair

◆使う物：ファンド、ベビーパウダー、スチール定規、カッター、彫塑べら、ABS板2mm、プラスチック棒2mmφ、3mmφ

◆Materials foundation clay, baby powder, steel ruler, cutter, modeling spatula, 2-mm ABS, 2-mm and 3-mm plastic rod

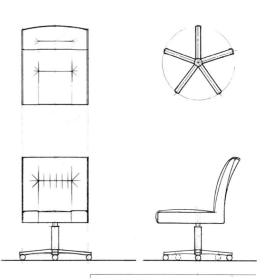

１．このような革張りの回転椅子を作ってみる。

1: Try making this type of leather upholstery swivel chair.

２．写真を元に図面をおこす。少しアレンジしてみた。

2: Create drawings based on the photo. The drawings were arranged a bit here.

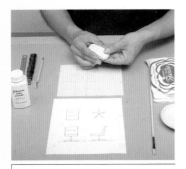

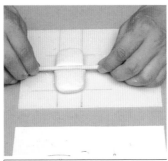

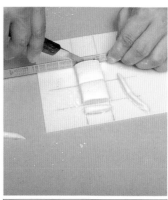

３．図面に合わせ、台に座と背の幅と奥行きを書いておく。ファンドを厚めにのばし、ベビーパウダーをかける。一定の厚みにのばせなかったらp.94-3を参照のこと。

3: Draw the width and depth of the seat and back according to the drawing. Stretch the clay into a thick slab and sprinkle on baby powder. See p.94-3.

４．型の上に乗せ板で上から押し、厚さを合わせながら平たくのばす。4mmの丸棒で座と背のつなぎ部分を半分位まで押す。

4: Place on the mold and push flat with a board from above, stretching to the right thickness. Push in the connecting part between the seat and back about halfway with a 4-mm round rod.

５．一度背を立てて角度を見る。曲がらない場合はもう一度棒で押す。

5: Stand the back and check the angles. If it is not curved, once more push with the rod.

６．型の線に合わせ定規を押しあててからカッターで切り離す。

6: Press a ruler against the mold lines and cut away with a cutter.

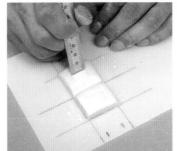

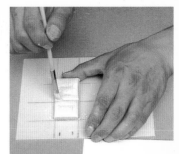

7．縦のくぼみを定規で軽く押し、跡をつける。

7: Press the vertical indentations lightly with a ruler and leave an impression.

8．横のくぼみも定規などで押し、跡をつける。

8: Do the same for the horizontal indentations.

9．彫塑べらで革の細かいくぼみを押してつける。

9: Use a modeling spatula to press in the fine indentations of the leather.

10．つなぎ部分に木工ボンドを塗り立ち上げる。

10: Apply wood bond to the connecting part and stand up.

11．背の丸みを指で整える。

11: Mold the roundness of the back with your fingers.

12．角度に合わせ立て掛けて、このまま1日乾かし変形しなくなったら取り外し、金網など風通しのよい物の上にのせさらに1日乾かす。

12: Adjust the angle and stand up. Let it dry this way for one day. When the shape is hardened, remove. Set on a metal screen, towel or other material that allows the air to flow around it, and let it dry for another day.

13．完全に乾いたらカッターで余分な部分をそぎ落とし、座と背を切り厚みを合わせる。

13: When it dries thoroughly, use a cutter to scrape off the excess. Cut the seat and back and match the thickness.

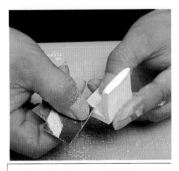

14．紙ヤスリを使い丸みをつける。

14: Use sandpaper to round it off.

15．つなぎ部分に大きな隙間ができたり削り過ぎた場合は、水をつけてから木工パテをへらで押し込むように埋める。ちょっとした隙間は水に溶いた木工パテを筆で塗る。

15: If there is a large gap where the parts connect or if you shaved too much off, wet first then press on wood putty with a spatula. For a small gap, brush on diluted wood putty with a brush.

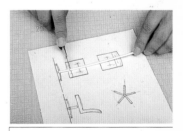

16．キャスター付き脚を作る。座の底に穴を開けて刺すのでその分長めに脚の志棒（プラスチック棒3mmφ）を切る。切り方はカッターを乗せてころがしながら切れ目を入れてから折る。

16: Make legs with casters. Since holes will be opened on the bottom of the seat to stick the caster on, leave that part long when cutting the 3-mm diameter plastic rod for the casters.
N.B. Place the blade of the cutter on the plastic rod and cut by rolling the rod.

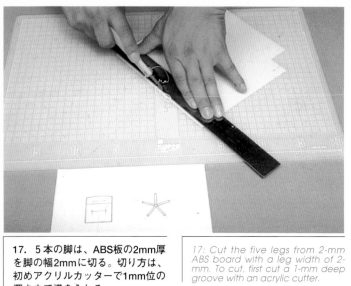

17. 5本の脚は、ABS板の2mm厚を脚の幅2mmに切る。切り方は、初めアクリルカッターで1mm位の深さまで溝を入れる。

17: Cut the five legs from 2-mm ABS board with a leg width of 2-mm. To cut, first cut a 1-mm deep groove with an acrylic cutter.

18. 溝に沿ってカッターで切る。こうすると厚手のABS板も容易に切ることができる。

18: Cut with a cutter along the groove. By using this method, even thick ABS board can be cut easily.

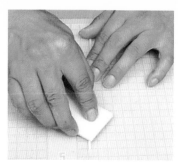

19. 角材になるよう直角に紙ヤスリをかける。

19: Sand to right angles with sandpaper.

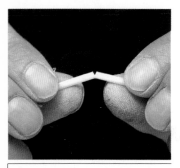

20. 脚の長さに合わせ切れ目を入れてから折る。

20: Put in a cut line to the length of the legs and bend.

21. 脚の先をカッターで削り、先細りにしてから紙ヤスリをかける。カッターで切り過ぎた場合は破片を戻しアクリダインで接着する。

21: Taper off the end of the leg with a cutter, then sand with sandpaper. If you cut off too much with the cutter, attach the fragments back on with acridine.

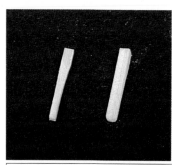

22. このようになればよい。

22: Try to make it look like the picture at left.

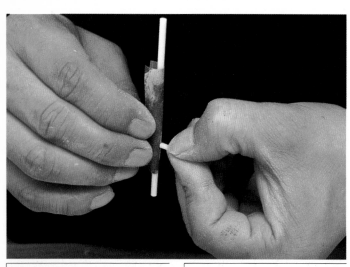

23. 志棒に接する面を志棒と同じ太さの棒に紙ヤスリを巻き付け丸くヤスリがけする。

23: To round off the parts that touch the plastic rod, wrap sandpaper around a rod the same thickness as the plastic rod and sand.

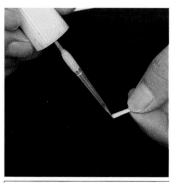

24. 接着面にアクリダインをつける。

24: Apply acridine to the contacting surfaces.

25. すぐに志棒につけ固まるのを待つ。志棒が垂直に立っているか確認する。

25: Stick to the plastic rod right away and wait for it to harden. Make sure that the plastic rod is standing perpendicular.

26. 5本つけたらもう一度アクリダインをたっぷりつけておく。

26: When all five legs have been attached, once more apply acridine liberally.

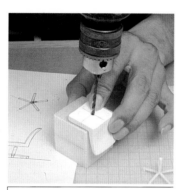

27. キャスターを作る。2mmのプラスチック棒を2mmの幅で切り出す。

27: Make the casters. Use 2-mm plastic rod cut to a width of 2-mm. Place the blade of the cutter on the plastic rod and cut by rolling the rod.

28. 脚の先にアクリダインをつけ、その上にキャスターを乗せ接着する。

28: Apply acridine to the bottom of the leg, and place the caster on top to attach.

29. このように作ればよい。

29: Make it to look like this.

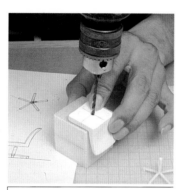

30. 座の底に2mmφの穴を厚さの半分位まで開ける。ドリルを使わなくてもドリルの刃だけを使って開けることができる。

30: Open a hole in the bottom of the seat about half of the 2-mm diameter. Even without using a drill, you can open the hole by turning the drill bit with your fingers.

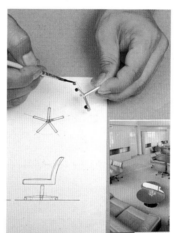

31. 塗装する。脚はシルバーの缶スプレーを塗り、乾いたらキャスター部分に黒のリキテックスを塗る。座は色に合わせ缶スプレーを塗る。色が合わない場合は2、3色を交互に塗るか、2本いっぺんに塗り色を合わせるとよい(p.28-24参照)。

31: Paint. Paint the legs with silver spray paint, and when it dries paint the casters with black liquitex. Spray the seat with a suitable color. When the color does not match, alternate two or three colors or paint two colors at once. See p.28-24.

32. 前。

32: The front.

33. 後ろ。座は八分程のツヤ位が革張りの感じになる。

33: The back. Approximately 80% gloss on the seat gives the feel of leather.

34. 出来上がり。

34: The finished model.

34

ソファーの作り方 I
ABS板で作るソファー　S=1/30
モデル／カッシーナ403Tilbury

How to Make a Sofa (I)
A sofa made from ABS board S = 1/30
Model: Catthina 403 Tilbury

◆使う物：ABS板かアクリル板（1mm、3mm）、糸のこ、スコヤ、スチール定規、カッター、三角形の金ヤスリ、アクリルカッター、アクリダイン、サーフェイサー、缶スプレー、スチのり

◆Materials: ABS or acrylic board (1-mm, 3-mm), fret saw, square, steel ruler, cutter, triangular metal file, acrylic cutter, acridine, surfacer, spray paint, spray glue

1．背と座のクッション部分になるアクリル板かABS板の3mm厚を用意する。それを図面を基に糸のこでちょうどいい大きさにカットする。それからクッション一つ一つの大きさに合わせアクリルカッターでV溝を入れる。

1: Prepare 3-mm thick acrylic board or ABS board for the back and seat cushion. Based on the drawing, cut with a fret saw to just the right size. Then matching the size of each cushion, cut in a V-groove with an acrylic cutter.

2．V溝に合わせ三角形の金ヤスリで削り、自然な感じの丸みを出す。

2: File along the V-groove with a triangular metal file to create a natural roundness.

3．クッションの外周の縁の部分も表面から裏面にかけてヤスリで丸みを出す。仕上げは紙ヤスリで。

3: File along the circumference of the edge of the cushion from front to back to bring out roundness.

4．次にクッションを乗せる外枠になるABS板1mm厚を用意する。背板1枚、肘掛け板2枚、座板1枚（補強材にもなる）計4枚を図面をあたってちょうどいい長さにカットする。切り方は定規をあて切れ目を入れて折れば簡単に切り出せる。

4: Next, prepare the external frame upon which the cushion will be set using 1-mm ABS board. Cut four pieces by laying against the drawing to get just the right length. One for the back, two for the armrests and one for the seat (to put cushions on and as reinforcing material). Press a ruler against the board and put in a cutting line with the cutter, then bend. In this way you can easily cut it away.

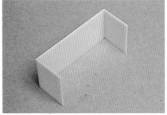

5．それをアクリダインで接着する。ここでは背板に肘掛け板をかぶせて接着してある。切り出しの時背の厚み分だけ多めに切るように注意する。

5: Attach these using acridine. Here, the boards for the armrests were attached covering the backboard. Make sure when cutting the back to make it a little thick.

6．座の受け材を接着する。固まったら四方を紙ヤスリをかけ丸みを出す。

6: Attach the seat support material. When it hardens, use sandpaper to smooth the projecting parts.

7．塗装する。各パーツにサーフェイサー（下地材）を塗り一度よく乾かし600番位の紙ヤスリをかけ小さな凹凸をなくす。次に仕上げ色を塗る。初め30cm位離して塗り、乾いたら50cm位離して上からかぶせるように塗る。こうすると布の感じが出せる。乾いたらスチのりで接着する。

7: Paint. Apply surfacer to each part (substrate material), dry thoroughly, then sand with approximately #600 sandpaper to eliminate the indentations and projections. Next, paint the finishing color. First paint from a distance of about 50-cm from above just to cover. This will bring out the feel of cloth.When it dries, glue on with styrene glue.

8．出来上がり。

8: The finished model.

35

ソファーの作り方 II
スチレンボードで作るソファー　S=1/20

How to Make a Sofa (II)
Making a sofa from styrene board S = 1/20

◆使う物：7mmスチレンボード、カッター、スチール定規、スコヤ、彫塑べら、紙ヤスリ、スチのり、木工パテ、プラモデル用サーフェイサー、面相筆、リキテックス

◆Materials: 7-mm styrene board, cutter, steel ruler, square, modeling spatula, sandpaper, styrene glue, wood putty, surfacer for plastic models and many colors of spray paint, fine brush, liquitex

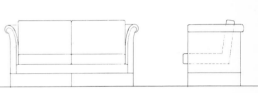

2．写真を元に図面をおこす。

2: Create drawings from the photo.

1．実物の写真。KOSUGA 6520LS

1: A photograph of the actual sofa. Kosuga 6520 LS

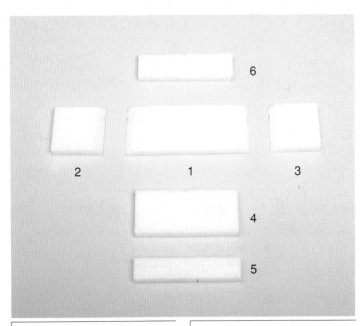

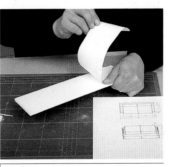

4．パーツの作り方（パーツ図1.2.3）7mmのスチレンボードを適当な大きさに切り、両面の紙を剥ぐ。

4: How to make the parts (Parts 1, 2 and 3). Cut 7-mm styrene board to roughly the right size, and peel off the paper from both sides.

5．背の丸みを作る。背の高さにカットしてから丸みの下にカッターで2、3mmの深さで切れ込みを入れる。

5: Make the curve of the back. First, cut with a cutter just 2-3 mm in below the curve.

3．各パーツ。1.背、2.3.側面（肘掛け）、4.座、5.座の受け材、6.背のクッション。

3: The various parts. 1 is the back, 2 and 3 the sides (armrests), 4 the seat, 5 the seat support material and 6 the back cushion.

7．このようにV溝に切る。

7: Cut in a V-groove in this way.

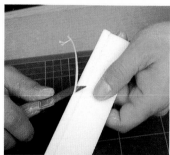

8．角をカッターで切り、丸みをつける。

8: Cut the corners with the cutter to round off.

6．今度は、カッターの刃を下の方向から、先に入れた切れ目まで入れる。
＊カッターの刃は30°の刃を使い、切れなくなったらまめに交換すること。

6: Next, cut from below to where you made the cut line previously. N.B. Use a 30-degree cutter blade and when it no longer cuts well, immediately break off to get a fresh blade.

9．溝に合わせ、240番位の紙ヤスリを使い下の部分を薄くする。ヤスリの作り方はp.10-1参照。

9: Along the groove, use #240 sandpaper or so to sand the lower part and make thinner. For how to sand, see p. 10-1.

10．この位まで薄くする。

10: Stop when you have sanded this much.

11．背のパーツ1．2．3を直角に切ってから、カッターで角を45°になるように少しずつそぐようにカットする。

11: After cutting the back parts 1, 2, and 3 at right angles, use a cutter at a 45-degree angle to scrape away little by little.

12．紙ヤスリで切り口を平らにし、接着面と合わせながら直角になるようにする。

12: Sand the cut edges flat. Align with the attached side, and sand to form a right angle.

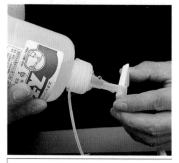

13．パーツが出来たら、両面にスチのりを塗る。

13: Attach. When the parts are done, apply styrene glue to both sides.

14．少し乾いたら組み立てる。

14: When it dries slightly, assemble.

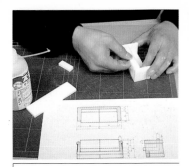

15. 座の受け材（パーツ図5）を取り付ける。図の右下赤線のパーツ。

15: Remove the seat support (5). This is the part on the lower right side of the drawing indicated by the red line.

16. 組み立てて乾いたらつなぎ部分をヤスリがけする。

16: After assembling, when it dries, file the connecting parts.

17. R部分もヤスリで丸みをつける。

17: File the curved section and round it off.

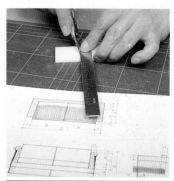

18. クッション（4.5）を作る。図に合わせパーツを切り出し、クッションの継ぎ目をV溝に1mm位の深さにカットする。

18: Make the cushions (4, 5). Align parts with drawing and cut out. Cut a V-groove at a depth of 1-mm or so to create the cushion seams.

19. 溝に合わせヤスリの角を使い、底から上にかけて丸みをつけながらかける。各コーナーも丸みをつけ、背も同じように作る。
＊紙ヤスリは初め240番位で、仕上げは600番位で。

19: Use the corner of the sandpaper along the groove to sand from the base to the top to round the edges. Sand the corners all around to create roundness.
N.B. First use #240 sandpaper, then finish with about #600.

20. スチのりで座と背のクッションを取り付ける。

20: Attach the seat and back with styrene glue.

21. スカートのひだの上部をカッターで1mm位の深さの切れ目を入れ一周する。

21: Use the cutter to put in a cut line about 1-mm deep on the upper part of the skirt pleats all the way around.

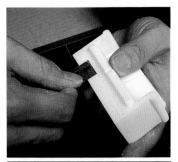

22. スチール定規でカットラインの下に合わせ押してしわをつける。

22: Line up a steel ruler below the cut line and press to create wrinkles.

23. 肘掛けの布の巻き込み部分を鉛筆で書くように溝をつけていく。

23: Dig a groove for the cloth wrap part of the armrest with a pencil.

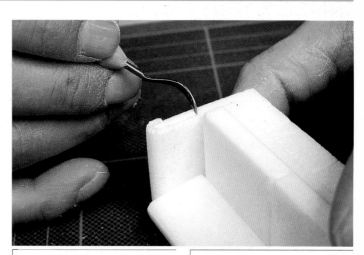

24. 先の尖った彫塑べらで押して、溝やしわをつける。

24: Press with a pointed-tip modeling spatula to make grooves and wrinkles.

25. 溝に沿ってヤスリの端で丸みをつける。

25: Sand along the grooves to create roundness.

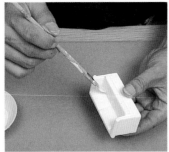

26. 木工パテを水で溶き（詳しくはp.14-9参照）筆で全体に塗る。乾いたら320番位の紙ヤスリで仕上げる。

26: Dilute wood putty with water (For more details see p. 14-9). Apply all over with a brush. When it dries, use about #320 sandpaper to do the finish sanding.

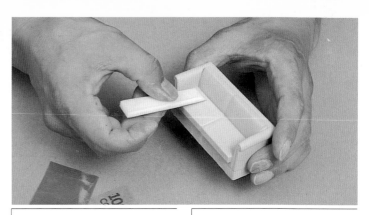

27. プラモデル用サーフェイサーを塗り、乾いたら600番位の紙ヤスリをすみずみまでかける。これをもう一度繰り返す。

27: Apply surfacer for plastic models and when it dries sand with about #600 from corner to corner. Apply again and sand once more. N.B. Cut the sandpaper to a suitable size. By cutting the edge or the side diagonally you can get into corners to sand.

28. 仕上げにサーフェイサーをもう一度塗って出来上がり。ここまで下地処理するとキズ一つなく仕上げられる。

28: For the finish, apply surfacer once more. By processing the substrate this much, the finish will show no marks or scratches.
*The surfacer used here was "Mr. Surfacer".

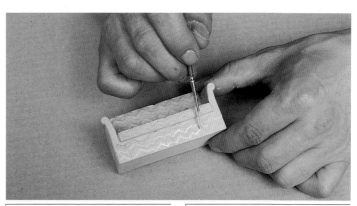

29. 下地塗装してから面相筆で模様を描く。まずプラモデル用缶スプレーの2、3色を使い色を合わせる。色が合わなかったら2本いっぺんに塗ると混ざりやすく中間色が出やすい。乾いたらリキテックスを面相筆で塗り模様を描く。

29: After painting the substrate, use a fine brush to draw on the pattern. Paint with spray used for plastic models, then use two or three colors of regular spray paint to adjust the color. If the color isn't right, painting two colors at once makes the colors blend easily to help bring out an intermediate tone. When this dries, use a fine brush to draw on the pattern with liquitex.

30. ぼかし塗装。模様が目立ち過ぎたら下地塗装で使った缶スプレーを50〜60cm離し、温めてからかぶせるように軽く塗る。

30: Gradation painting. If the pattern stands out too much, spray the color used for the substrate at a distance of 50-60 cm to cover lightly.

31. ぼかし塗装の効果。左はぼかし前、右は下地塗装に使ったスプレーをもう一度塗り、ぼかしてある。

31: The effect of gradation painting. On the left is before gradation painting. On the right is after the color used for the substrate is sprayed on again.

32. 出来上がり。

32: The finished model.

36

ソファーの作り方 Ⅲ
How to Make a Sofa (III)

◆使う物：スチレンペーパー3mm・5mm、カッター、スチール定規、木工パテ、紙ヤスリ、スチのり、彫塑べら、プラスチック棒3mm角、ニッパ、プラモデル用サーフェイサー及び各色缶スプレー

◆Materials: 3-mm and 5-mm styrene paper, cutter, steel ruler, wood putty, sandpaper, styrene glue, modeling spatula, plastic 3-mm square bar, nipper, surfacer for plastic models, and many colors of spray paint

１．これから作るソファーの実物写真。ソファーの作り方Ⅱと違い、背のコーナーが大きくRになっているのに注意。
IPS-14 STANDARD SOFA

1: This is the sofa we are going to make. It has a different back from Sofa II, the corners are larger and have a curved shape.

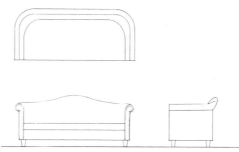

２．写真から図面をおこす。

2: Create drawings from the photograph.

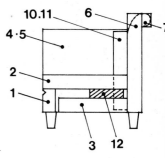

３．断面図。次の４と照らし合わせてみていただきたい。

3: A cross-section. Please view with Step 4 below.

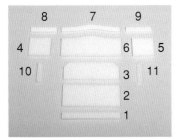

４．各パーツ。1.座の受け材、2.座面、3.側面（肘掛け）と背の補強材、4.5.側面（肘掛け）、6.背板、7.背の上部の丸み材、8.9.肘掛けの丸み材、10.11.背のコーナーの補強材（三角形）。

4: The parts: 1. Seat support material; 2. Seat surface; 3. Side (armrest) and back reinforcement material; 4, 5. Side (armrest); 6. Backboard; 7. Rounded material of upper part of back; 8 & 9. Rounded material of armrest; 10, 11. Back corner reinforcement material (triangular)

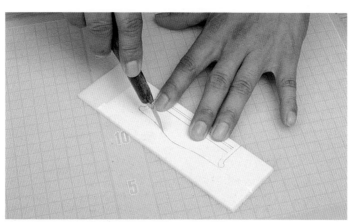

５．背（6）を作る。スチレンペーパー5mmに図面のコピーを背の形に切り出し、それをスプレーのりで貼りつける。図面に合わせ曲面はフリーハンドでカットする。上の赤丸の部分の出っ張りはまっすぐに切る。

5: Make the back (6).Lay 5-mm styrene paper on a copy of the drawing and cut out to the shape of the back, then paste with spray glue. According to the drawing, cut the curved parts freehand. Cut straight the upper part circled in red that sticks out.

６．丸み材（7）を作る。5で切り出した背（6）をゲージに、スチレンペーパー3mm厚の上に乗せて上をカットする。

6: Make the rounded material (7). Using the back (6) cut out in Step 5 as a gauge, lay onto 3-mm styrene paper and cut the top.

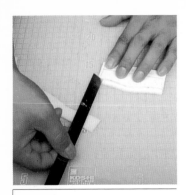

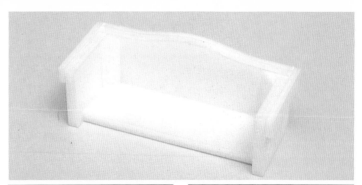

7．背の丸み材（7）の高さに合わせ（6）のゲージをずらす。

7: Align to the height of the back's rounded material and slide the gauge.

8．背（6）をゲージにしてカッターで切る。その他のパーツはスコヤを使い、直角に切り出す。（10．11）の補強材は5mm厚のスチレンペーパーを使い三角形に切り出す。

8: Using the back (6) as a gauge, cut with the cutter. Cut out the other parts at right angles using a square. Cut out the reinforcement material (10, 11) from 5-mm styrene paper in a triangular shape.

9．パーツをスチのりで組み立てる。（6）に（4.5）をツキツケで接着し、つまり（4.5）の厚み分大きくなっている。三角形の補強材（10.11）をコーナーにしっかりつける。背と側面が変形しないように補強材（3）を取り付ける。次に（7.8.9）の丸み材をつける。時間をかけ固まるのを待つ。スチのりは両面塗り、半乾きになってから貼る。

9: Assemble the parts with styrene glue.Connect part 6 and 4, 5 with a little force. In other words, the thick part of 4, 5 gets larger. Attach the triangular reinforcement material (10, 11) firmly to the corners. Attach reinforcement material (3) to make sure the back and sides don't cave in. Next, attach the rounded material (7, 8, 9). Let it sit until everything hardens.
N.B. Apply styrene glue to both sides and paste together when the glue is half-dry.

10．十分に固まったらコーナーをカットし、丸みを図面に合わせる。丸み材の出はRに合わせて左右バランスよくカットする。

10: Cut the corners.When it has hardened adequately, cut the corners, and adjust the roundness according to the drawings. Align the extended part of the rounded material with the curve and cut to achieve a good balance between right and left.

11．丸み材の角はカッターでそぐように切り、丸みをつける。

11: Scrape the corner of the rounded material with the cutter to round off.

12．内側の丸みもカッターで切る。

12: Use the cutter also to round off the inside.

13．240番位の紙ヤスリを粗くかけて、形を整える。

13: Sand with sandpaper.
File roughly with approximately #240 sandpaper to produce the general shape.

14．コーナーは木工パテの原液をへらで盛る。盛り過ぎるとなかなか乾かなかったり、割れが入るので少しずつ2、3回に分けて盛るとよい。石膏を混ぜてもよい。（p. 15-10 参照）

14: Stack wood putty.
Stack undiluted wood putty with a spatula to make the corner.
N.B. If you stack up too much at once, it takes too long to dry and can crack, so it is better to layer it on two or three times. Or mix with plaster (See p. 15-10).

15．木工パテに水を少し入れ全体にハケ塗りする。（p.14-9 参照）

15: Apply diluted putty. Mix a little water with wood putty and brush on (See p. 14-9).
N.B. If using an electric dryer, dry at a distance.

16. 完全に乾いたら紙ヤスリの240番を使いゆっくり形を整える。

16: Sand down the putty. When it dries completely, sand to shape with #240 sandpaper. Take your time in sanding.

17. 座（2）を切り出す。背のRに合わせながら少しずつカットしていく。

17: Cut out the seat (2). Cut little by little in line with the curve of the back.

18. 微妙な調整は紙ヤスリで行う。

18: Make fine adjustments with sandpaper.

19. 座の受け（1）を取り付ける。受け材が固まったら座面のコーナーをカッターで切り、丸みをつける。

19: Attach the seat support (1). When the support material hardens, cut the corners of the seat surface with the cutter to round off.

20. 紙ヤスリで丸みをきれいにする。特に接着面を平らにしておく。

20: Smooth the rounded parts with sandpaper. Particularly sand the attached part flat.

21. 座面の厚みの溝をカッターでV溝にカットする。

21: Cut a V-groove with a cutter into the thick groove of the seat surface.

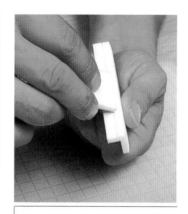

22. V溝に合わせヤスリの角で丸みをつける。

22: Round with the corner of a piece of sandpaper along the V-groove.

23. 15と同じように木工パテを塗る。

23: Apply wood putty as in Step 15.

24. 乾いたら紙ヤスリをかける。溝を処理する時は紙ヤスリを折って使うとよい。

24: When this dries, sand with sandpaper. When filing the groove, it is a good idea to fold the sandpaper.

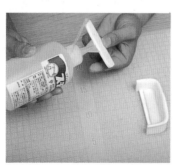

25. 座面を取り付ける。上のように座が水平になるように高さ調整材（12）を入れてから接点にスチのりを少しつけ取り付ける。

25: Attach the seat surface. As above, insert the height-adjusting material (12) to make the seat level, then apply a little styrene glue to the contact points and attach.

26. 側面との隙間は、木工パテの原液をへらで押し込むように埋める。

26: Press undiluted wood putty into the space on the sides.

27. ちょっとした隙間は水で溶いた木工パテを面相筆につけ塗る。

27: For tiny gaps, use diluted wood putty and apply with a fine brush.

28. 塗った後、すぐに丸めたティッシュペーパーに水をつけ、端から拭き取る。こうするとヤスリを使わずに仕上がる。

28: Immediately after applying, ball up a tissue, dip it in water and wipe away from the edges. This way, finishing is done without sanding.

29. 布の巻き込みの溝を入れる。水を筆で塗ってから鉛筆で書くように溝を掘る。直線は定規を使う。
＊ソファーの作り方Ⅱと溝を入れるタイミングが違うのは、溝が浅いため後でパテを塗ると埋まってしまうため。

29: Cut in the groove for the cloth roll. Apply water with a brush and dig in a groove with a pencil. To get a straight line, use a ruler. N.B. This groove differs from the groove in Sofa II in that it is shallow, so that when you putty it in later, it covers up the groove.

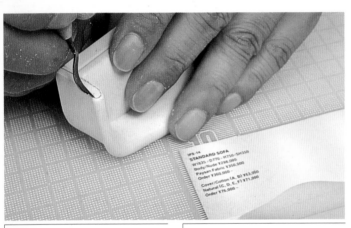

30. 線に合わせ布のシワをへらで軽く押し、溝を作る。水をつけていないと割れてしまうので注意。乾いたら軽くヤスリをかける。

30: Along the lines, press wrinkles lightly with the spatula to make grooves. N.B. If you don't wet the surface, the putty will crack. When the water dries, shape by sanding lightly with the corner of sand-paper.

31. 脚を作る。プラスチック棒かABS板の角材をカッターで先細りにする。

31: Make the legs. Use square plastic rod or ABS board and taper the ends with a cutter.

32. 切り口に紙ヤスリをかける。

32: Sand the edges with sand-paper.

33. ニッパか糸のこで長さに合わせて切る。切り口はヤスリで平らにしておく。

33: Align to the proper length and cut with a nipper or fret saw. Sand the edges flat with sandpaper.

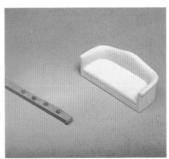

34. 各部分ごとに塗装する。ソファーの布地塗装はp.61-25、26参照。

34: Paint each part. For painting the sofa cloth see p. 61-25,26.

35. 出来上がり。

35: The finished model.

座面をスチレンペーパーで作り、ファンドを薄く伸ばしてから座に巻き固める。それから削り出して作る。

Make the seat from styrene paper, thinly stretching the clay over the seat. Then trim and form.

テーブルのガラスはタペストリー加工してある。(p.120-59参照)

The table glass uses tapestry processing. (See p. 120-59)

S＝1/50の家具。左から座を作り、ファンドを巻き固めてから削り出す。2番目はスチレンペーパーで作り、3番目はABS板で下地を作り、ファンドでレザー風に仕上げた。

Furniture at a scale of 1/50. From the left, the first photo shows the seat with the clay stretched over it, after being trimmed and formed. The second photo shows the model made from styrene paper and the third shows the substrate made from ABS board, finished with foundation clay to look like leather.

38

什器の作り方
How to Make a Cabinet

◆**使う物**：ABS板1mm厚、カッター、アクリルカッター、スチール定規、スコヤ、紙ヤスリ、アクリル板0.5mm、アクリダイン、リキテックス、サーフェイサー、ICテープ、ポンチ1mmφ

◆**Materials**: 1-mm ABS board, cutter, acrylic cutter, steel ruler, square, sandpaper, 0.5-mm acrylic board, acridine, liquitex, surfacer, IC tape, 1-mm diameter hole puncher

1．これから作るキャビネットの写真。　　IDEE IPX-05

1: A picture of the cabinet we are going to make.　IDEE IPX-05

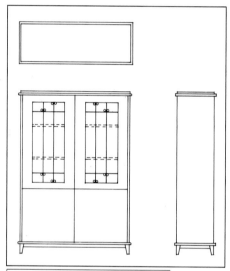

2．写真から図面をおこす。

2: Create drawings from the photo.

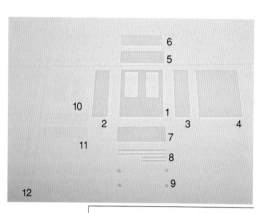

3．(1)前扉、(2)(3)側面、(4)背板、(5)(6)天板、(7)底板、(8)脚の補強材、(9)脚、(10)扉のガラス、(11)ガラス棚、(12)ガラス取り付け用押さえ縁。

3: 1. Front door; 2, 3. Sideboards; 4. Backboard; 5, 6. Top; 7. Bottom; 8. Reinforcing material for legs; 9. Legs; 10. Door glass; 11. Glass shelf; 12. Molding for attaching glass

4．図面を元にABS板1mmを切り出し(1)、ガラス部分をカッターで切れ目を入れ、鉛筆の粉をティッシュでこすり、線を明確にする。
＊扉は閉じた状態であればこのように1枚にして作るとよい。

4: Cut the 1-mm ABS board according to the drawing (1), score a cut line on the glass using the cutter and rub on pencil lead with a tissue to make the line more visible.
N.B. If the doors are to be closed, it is good to make this from a single sheet.

5．扉のスリ部分をアクリルカッターでV溝を入れる。

5: Notch a V-groove with the acrylic cutter for the glass part of the door.

6．印より1mm位内側にカッターで切れ目を入れ一周する。

6: About 1 mm inside the mark, score a cut line all the way around with the cutter.

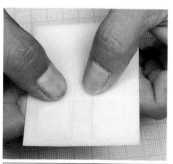

7．裏から切れ目に合わせ指で軽く押すと白い線が出る。

7: Align with the cut line from the back, press lightly with your finger and a white line will appear.

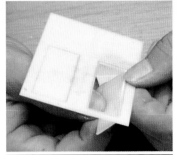

8．白い線が出たら、それに合わせ裏からもカッターで切れ目を入れる。これでだいたい切り抜くことができる。片面からだけでは切り抜くことがむずかしいため。

8: When the white line appears, score a cut line from the back along this line with the cutter. You can pretty much cut it out by now. If you cut only one side, it will be difficult to cut out entirely.

9．指で押して抜く。このように1mm内側で抜くのは切りすぎたり切り口が斜めになったりするので、初めに少し内側で抜いておく。

9: Press through with your fingers. Press just a little toward the inside at first using the 1 mm allowance to avoid cutting too much, also preventing the edge from becoming slanted.

10．中が抜けたら線にカッターの刃を合わせて切る。こうすると簡単にカッターで切ることができ、なおかつ切り口がきれいになる。

10: When the center is out, cut along the line with the blade of the cutter. Now the cutter should cut easily and you can sharpen the edges.

11．切り口をヤスリがけする。紙ヤスリを削る幅に合わせてカットして使うと、コーナーまできれいに仕上がる。(ヤスリの作り方はp.10-1参照)

11: Sand the edges. Cut the sandpaper to the width to be sanded so that you can sand perfectly to the corners. (For how to sand, see p. 10-1)

12．ガラスをはめ込むための押さえ(12)0.3mm〜0.5mm厚のアクリル板を適当な幅に切り、裏から0.5mm位出して、四方に回しひっかかりを作る。

12: Cut 0.3-mm to 0.5-mm acrylic board to a suitable width for the molding (12) into which to set the glass. Let about 0.5 mm stick out from the back, rotate all around and make a knob to serve as a catch.

13．側板(2・3)を切り出してから、ガラス棚の取り付け位置を側板(2・3)をテープで止め、いっぺんにカッターで印をつける。

13: After cutting out the sideboards(2, 3), fasten them to the place where the glass shelf will be attached and make a temporary mark there with the cutter.

14．鉛筆の粉をティッシュですりこんで見やすくする。

14: Rub on pencil lead with a tissue to make the lines more visible.

15．側板(2・3)と背板(4)を接着して、扉(1)をテープで止めセットしてから天板(5)と底板(7)を接着する。
＊扉(1)をセットしないで天板と底板を接着すると扉が入らなかったり、隙間ができたりするので注意。

15: Attach the sideboards(2, 3) to the backboard(4), fasten the door (1) with tape and set before attaching the top (5) and bottom (7).
N.B. If you attach the top and bottom without setting the door (1), the door will not fit in or a gap will be left.

16．扉の押さえ板をつける。0.5mmのアクリル板を扉の厚み分だけ減らして上下に取り付ける。これを付けることにより扉が奥に入りすぎるのを止める。

16: Attach the door stopper. Leave just enough room for the thickness of the door with the 0.5-mm acrylic board and attach on top and bottom. By attaching, it stops the door from going in too deep.

17．ガラス棚の受けを付ける。1mmのABS板を2mm位の幅にカットし、扉の内側におさまる長さでカットし13で付けた印に合わせ接着する。

17: Attach the glass shelf support. Cut 1-mm ABS board about 2 mm wide, and cut to a length that fits on the inside of the door. Align with the mark made in Step 13 and attach.

18．脚を取り付ける。脚は図のように2面が斜めになっているのでプラスチック棒などの角材をヤスリがけして2面を斜めにしてから、長さに合わせてニッパー又は糸ノコでカットし、切り口をヤスリがけして4本の長さを合わせる。

18: Attach the legs. As shown in the drawing, two sides of the legs are slanted, so after sanding the plastic rod (or similar square material) and making the two sides slanted, use a nipper or fret saw to cut, then sand the edges and match up the lengths of the four legs.

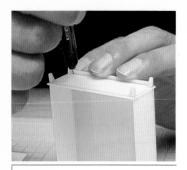 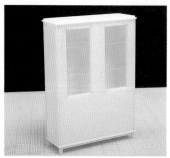  

19．ABS板をカットして作った補
強材（8）を斜めにカットした部分
にあて、マジックで印を付けカッ
ターでカットし、アクリダインで
接着する。

*19: Place the reinforcing material
(8) cut from ABS board against the
slanted part, mark with a marker,
cut with the cutter and attach with
acridine.*

20．組み立てた状態。
ガラス棚は0.5mmのアクリル透明
板で作る。扉とガラス棚はまだ接
着しないように。

*20: After assembly. Make the glass
shelf from 0.5-mm transparent
acrylic board. Do not attach the
doors and the glass shelf yet.*

21．塗装する。
サーフェイサーで下地塗りをする。

*21: Paint. Apply surfacer as a
substrate.*

22．リキテックスで色を付ける。
塗料は乾くと色が変わるので一度
乾かした状態を見てみる。初めは
濃いめのリキテックスでよく伸ば
し塗り、よく乾かす。

*22: Color with liquitex. When the
paint dries it changes color, so
wait until it dries before checking
the color. First spread on a dark-
colored liquitex well and let dry
thoroughly.*

 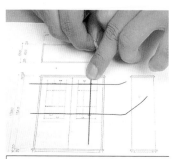  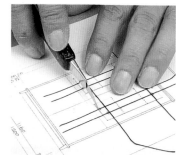

23．2回目は白を少し入れ、水も
多めにして薄く塗ると筆のムラが
出て、板目風に見える。

*23: The second time, mix in a bit of
white and dilute with a lot water.
When you apply lightly, the
irregularity of the brush makes it
look like wood grain.*

24．ガラス面の装飾金物を作る。
写真のように金物をまねてみる。
ガラスの板（10）を図の上におき、
ICテープ0.5mmを金物の線に合わ
せ貼る。

*24: Make the decorative metal for
the glass. Imitate the metal shown
in the picture. Place the glass
sheet (10) on the drawing, and
stick on 0.5-mm IC tape along the
line of the metal strip.*

25．クロスした部分は、上に乗っ
ているテープを平刃かカッターで
押し切りする。切った部分は取り
除く。こうするとかぶりもなく平
らになる。

*25: Where the tape crosses itself,
place a flat blade or cutter on top
and press to cut. Remove the cut
part. This way, it lays flat.*

26．板の端はカッターで押し切り
する。

*26: Press on the ends with the
cutter to cut.*

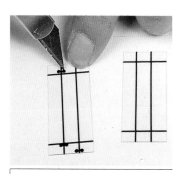 

27．写真のような丸い飾りを作る。
丸い物なのでカッティングシート
の黒を1mmφのポンチで抜いて
作ってみる。カッティングシート
がない場合は、マスキングテープ
に黒の塗装をしたものを使っても
よい。

*27: Make a round decoration as
shown in the photo. Since it is
round, try punching out a 1-mm
diameter hole from a black cutting
sheet. If you don't have a cutting
sheet, it is alright to use masking
tape painted black.*

28．写真に合わせて貼る。

*28: Match with the photo and
paste on.*

29．出来上がり。
扉とガラスはスチのり(p.12-5参照)
で軽く止める。

*29: The finished model. Lightly fix
the door and glass in place with
styrene glue(See p. 12-5).*

什器の作品例
Examples of Cabinets

１．ABS板１mmで組み立てた机。脚はプラスチック棒を先細りにしてある。

1: A desk assembled from 1-mm ABS board. The legs are plastic rods with the ends tapered.

２．同じくABS板で組んだキャビネット。細い面縁はABS板１mmを0.5mmに切り、アクリダインで接着してある。引き手金物は、真ちゅう棒を曲げて作ってある。

2: A cabinet, also assembled from ABS board. The narrow trim is made from 1-mm ABS board cut to 0.5 mm and attached with acridine. The metal handle is made by bending a brass rod.

３．セッティング例。

3: Example of a setting.

キッチンの作り方
How to Make a Kitchen

◆使う物：ABS板1mm、スチール定規、スコヤ、アクリル
カッター、カッター、ポンチ、アクリダイン、リキテックス、
鉄線、缶スプレー

◆**Materials**: 1-mm ABS board, steel ruler, square, acrylic
cutter, cutter, hole puncher, acridine, liquitex, steel wire,
spray paint

1．本物のキッチンの写真。
（株）ハウゼのシステムキッチンを
モデルに模型を作ってみる。縮小
率は1/30。カウンタートップは人
造大理石。扉は木目の染色仕上げ
を想定している。

*1: A photo of the actual kitchen.
Let's try making a model based on
this Howze   system kitchen unit.
The scale is 1/30. It is assumed that
the countertop is artificial marble
and the doors are stained wood.*

2．まずカウンターを作る。ABS
板1mmを寸法通りの大きさにカ
ットする。

*2: First make the counter. Cut 1-
mm ABS board to the proper
dimensions.*

3．カウンタートップに四角い穴
を2つ開ける。1つはシンク、も
う1つはクックトップを埋め込む
ための穴である。

*3: Open two square holes in the
countertop, one for the sink and
one to hold the stovetop.*

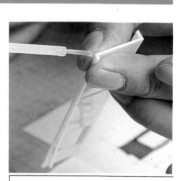

4．ABS板を細長くカットしてカ
ウンタートップの立ち上がり部分
を作る。

*4: Cut ABS board long and thin for
the part of the countertop that
stands.*

5．カットしたものをアクリダイ
ンでカウンタートップに接着する。

*5: Attach that to the countertop
with acridine.*

6．同様にカウンタートップの手
前の折り返し部分をABS板で作り、
アクリダインで接着する。

*6: In the same manner, make the
folded down front of the
countertop from ABS board and
attach also with acridine.*

7．3で開けた2つの穴の断面と、5と6で接着したところを紙ヤスリできれいに仕上げ、コーナーは丸みをつける。

7: Sand the section where the two holes were opened in Step 3 and the areas attached in Steps 5 and 6 until they are smooth and round the corners.

8．次にABS板でベースキャビネットの下地を作る。あとで前面に扉が付くのでその厚み分小さく作る。

8: Next, make the substrate for the base cabinet from ABS board. Since the doors will go on the front later, do not make it too thick.

9．シンクをABS板で組み立てる。シンクの穴と同寸の底板を作り深さに合わせ側板を4面巻くように取り付ける。(3で切り出した残材を使ってもよい)

9: Next, assemble the sink from ABS board. Make the base board of the sink the same size as the sink hole and attach the four side boards as if wrapping according to the depth of the sink (It is alright to use the material left over from Step 3).

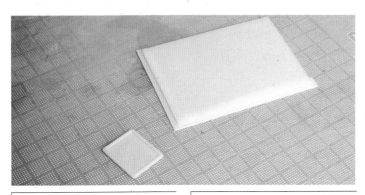

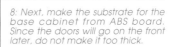

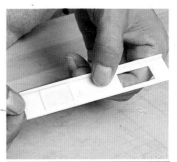

10．クックトップを作る。
これも3で切り出した残材を使い、4辺に細長く切ったABS板を、少しはみ出させて接着する。後でカウンタートップにはめ込んだ時、この棒がひっかかりになる。右上は分かりやすいように大きく作ったもので、裏返しにしてある。

10: Make the stovetop. Also use the leftover material from Step 3. Cut ABS board in four long, thin pieces, and attach, letting them stick out a little. Later, when it is fit into the countertop, these rods will serve as catches. On the upper right it was made large here to be easy to understand, and is turned inside out.

11．後でこのようにはめ込む。

11: Later, fit in like this.

12．扉を作る。
ABS板でベースキャビネットとウォールキャビネットの扉を作る。まずアクリルカッターで扉の目地をV溝に入れる。ここでは上と下の扉の目地をいっぺんに入れる。こうすると上と下の扉の目地がそろう。

12: Make the doors for the base cabinet and wall cabinet from ABS board. First, in the joints for the doors, notch a V-groove with an acrylic cutter. Notch both the upper and lower doors at the same time. This way they will line up.

13．キャビネットの上と下をカッターで切り出す。切り方は軽くカッターで切れ目を入れ、折れば簡単に切り離せる。

13: Cut away the top and bottom of the cabinet with the cutter. Lightly score a cut line with the cutter, and when bent, it should break free easily.

14．キャビネットの引き出しの線をアクリルカッターでV溝に入れる。ウォールキャビネットのフード上の線も入れる。

14: Cut in a V-groove with the acrylic cutter along the lines for the cabinet drawers. Notch the line for hood of the wall cabinet.

15．扉をベースキャビネットに合わせてみたところ。鉛筆で指したところが巾木になる。カウンタートップが扉と合うように注意する。

15: The model shown after aligning the doors with the base cabinet. The pencil points to the baseboard. Make sure the countertop lines up with the doors.

16．ウォールキャビネットに扉を付ける。
下地はABS板で組み、中心に1枚ブレ止めを入れる。

16: Attach the doors to the wall cabinet. Assemble the substrate from ABS board and in the center put one sheet to prevent slippage.

17．クックトップの火口を作る。ABS板をポンチで打ち抜き、丸い平らな板を2枚用意する。

17: Next, make the stovetop burner. Punch a hole in ABS board, and prepare two circles of flat board.

18．この2つの火口を10で作ったクックトップにアクリダインで接着する。

18: Attach these two burners with acridine to the stovetop you made in Step 10.

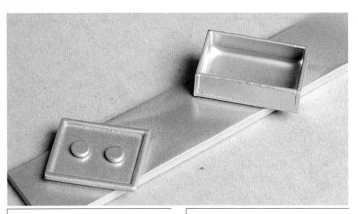

19．シンクとクックトップはステンレスを想定しているので、シルバーの缶スプレーを塗る。シンクの内側にはスプレーを多めにかける。こうすると四隅に塗料がたまり、自然な丸みが出て本物らしく見える。

19: The sink and stovetop are assumed to be stainless steel, so paint with silver spray paint. Spray a lot on the inside of the sink so that the paint collects in the four corners and creates a natural roundness that looks quite realistic.

20．カウンタートップにクリーム色の缶スプレーをかける。

20: Spray a cream color on the countertop.

21．染色仕上げを想定したキャビネットの扉を塗装する。
まずリキテックスをモデルの色より少し濃い色で木目方向に塗る。

21: Paint the doors of the cabinet where a stained finish is assumed. First paint on liquitex (with the grain) that is slightly darker than the model color.

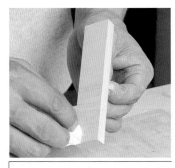

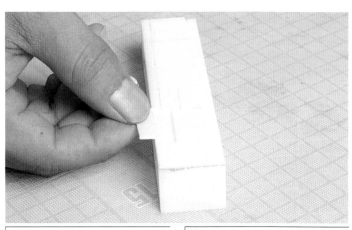

22．十分乾かしてから少し白を混ぜ、もう一度塗る。

22: After drying thoroughly, mix in a little white and paint again.

23．乾く前にティッシュで軽くふき取る。木目方向にふくこと。

23: Before it dries, wipe lightly with a tissue. Wipe with the grain of the wood.

24．ベースキャビネットの扉も同じように塗るが、その前に魚焼きグリルの扉をカッターでカットして外す。この部分は別の色（黒）で塗るため。

24: Paint the doors of the base cabinet in the same way, but before doing so, cut the grill door with the cutter and remove. This part will be painted a different color (black).

25. カットしたら21〜23と同じように リキテックスで塗る。巾木部分は別の色を塗る。

25: After it is cut, paint with liquitex as shown in Steps 21-23. Paint the baseboard a different color.

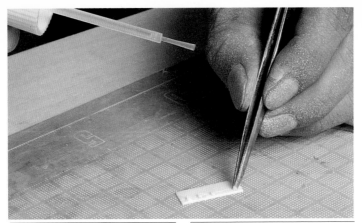

26. 魚焼きグリルの扉の上部につまみを取り付ける。
ABS板をポンチで抜き、アクリダインで接着する。

26: Attach a holder to the top of the grill door. Open a hole in ABS board with a hole puncher and attach with acridine.

27. クックトップの上につける前縁を作る。
鉄線をABS板などで作った「型」でコの字に曲げ、ニッパで型に合わせ切る。

27: Make the front rim for the stovetop. Make the steel lines by bending the "mold" made from ABS board into a squared "U" and adjust the shape with the nipper.

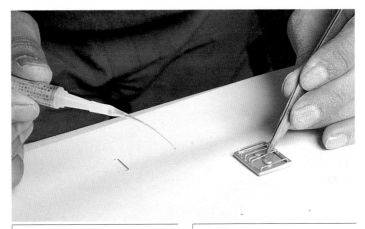

28. それを瞬間接着剤でクックプレートに接着する。接着面が汚くなったらもう一度缶スプレーで塗ってもよい。

28: Attach to the stove plate with instant bond. If the attaching surface gets dirty, it is alright to spray again with paint.

29. カウンタートップにシンクとクックトップをはめ込んだところ。

29: The sink and stovetop, after being fitted into the countertop.

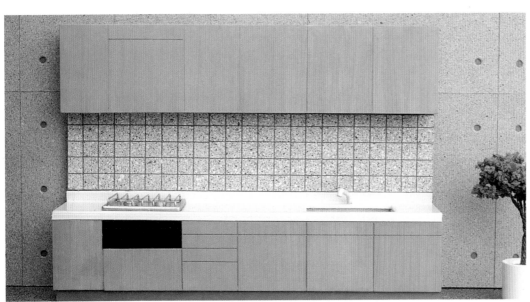

30. 出来上がり。

30: The finished model.

31. 住宅模型のキッチン部分。
S=1/10

31: The unit for a house model. S = 1/10

クッションの作り方 Ⅰ
ソファーに立て掛けるフリル付きクッションを作る。

How to Make a Cushion (I)
Making a cushion with frills to place on a sofa.

◆使う物：ファンド、ベビーパウダー、スチール定規、彫塑べら、カッター、下敷き（ABS板か塩ビ板）

◆Materials: foundation clay, baby powder, steel ruler, modeling spatula, cutter, substrate (ABS or vinyl chloride board)

１．ファンドを丸めベビーパウダーを付ける。
下敷きにするABS板か塩ビ板を用意し、板に作る大きさでゲージを書く。線は長めにし、ゲージの黄色の部分はクッションで縁がフリル部分である。

1: Make the foundation clay round and sprinkle with baby powder. Prepare ABS board or vinyl chloride board for the substrate. Draw a gauge for the size of board you will make. Extend the lines. The yellow part of the gauge will be the cushion and the bordering part will be the frills.

２．中央に厚みをつけ広げる。

2: Make it thick in the center and spread.

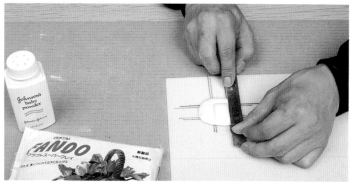

３．ゲージにベビーパウダーをふりかけ、ファンドをのせ、フリル部分の厚みを薄くする。（縁の部分）

3: Sprinkle baby powder on the gauge, place the clay on top, and press the flat part of a steel ruler along the frill border to thin that area (the bordering part).

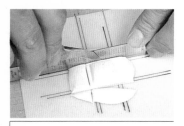

４．外の線に合わせてスチール定規を押し、カッターで切り取る。定規で押さえないで切ると変形してしまうので注意。

4: Align with the outside line, press with the steel ruler, and cut with the cutter. If you cut without holding down with the ruler, the shape will change.

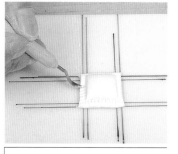

５．彫塑べらで押し、フリルを作る。このまま乾かすと平らなまま固まってしまう。

5: Press with a modeling spatula to make the frills. If you let it dry now, it will harden flat as it lays.

６．そこでソファーに使う場合は使う位置に置き、形を整えてこのまま固まるまで乾かす。

6: If you are using the cushion for a sofa, place it where it will sit and adjust the shape, then let it dry until it hardens.

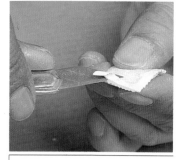

７．乾いたらフリル部分を裏から薄くする。

7: When it dries, thin the frill part from behind.

8: To make it look more realistic, line up the gathers of the frill and cut from behind to make thinner. Next, use a file to round the edges of the cushion.

８．もっと本物らしくするには、フリルのギザギザに合わせ裏からカッターで切り、薄くする。次にヤスリでクッション部分を削り丸みをつける。

９．出来上がり。

9: The finished model.

クッションの作り方 II（へそ付き）

ボタン（へそ）付きの
クッションの作り方。

How to Make a Cushion (II) (with indentation)

Making a cushion with button (indentation)

◆使う物：ファンド、ベビーパウダー、スチール定規、彫塑べら、カッター、ポンチ、下敷き（ABS板など）

◆**Materials**: foundation clay, baby powder, steel ruler, modeling spatula, cutter, hole puncher, substrate (ABS board, etc.)

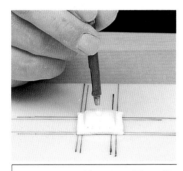

１．前のページの５まで同じ工程で進め、ポンチで中心を軽く押しボタンの跡をつける。ポンチがない場合は、ボールペンの芯を抜いた先で押してもよい。

1: Use the same process as on the previous page up to Step 5, then use a hole puncher, lightly pressing in the center to leave an impression. If you do not have a hole puncher, remove the ink tube from a ball-point pen and press with the end.

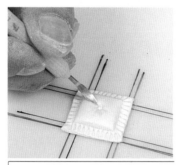

２．彫塑べらでシワをつける。

2: Make wrinkles with a modeling spatula.

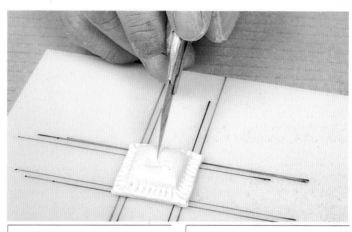

３．シワとシワの中間にカッターでさらに押し跡をつける。こうするとより本物らしくなる。

3: Between each of the wrinkles, press with a cutter to leave an impression. Doing so makes the model look more realistic.

４．使う場所に置き乾かす。固まったら軽くヤスリをかける。

4: Place in the position it is to be used and let dry. When it hardens, lightly file.

５．出来上がり。

5: The finished model. You can use either liquitex or spray paint to color it. For the painting method see p. 61, 25-26.

６．仕上げ。
缶スプレーで塗ってからパールの缶スプレーを塗ってコールテンの質感を出してみた。日本ペイントのシルキーパール使用。

6: Finish. After spraying with paint, pearl is sprayed on to bring out a golden quality. Nihon Paint's "Silky Pearl" is used here.

座布団の作り方
How to Make a Zabuton (floor cushion)

◆使う物：ファンド、ベビーパウダー、彫塑べら、カッター、スチール定規、細いひも、木工ボンド、下敷き（ABS板など）

◆**Materials:** foundation clay, baby powder, modeling spatula, steel ruler, thin string, wood bond, substrate (ABS board, etc.)

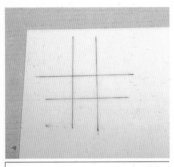

１．ABS板や厚紙などに座布団の大きさを書く。線は長めに、このゲージを作ると同じものが何個もできる。ここではS＝1/20で作る。

1: Draw the size of the zabuton on ABS board or thick paper. Draw the lines a little long, and using this gauge any number can be made. Here the scale used is 1/20.

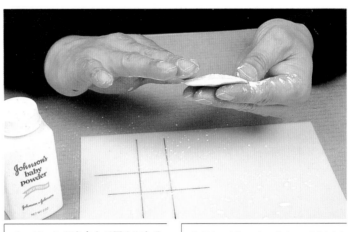

２．ファンドを中心が厚めになるように平らに延ばし、ベビーパウダーをつける。

2: Extend the clay flat, and thick in the center. Sprinkle on baby powder.

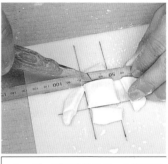

３．ゲージに乗せスチール定規で押してから内側にカッターを入れて切る。

3: Lay the steel ruler on this gauge and press. Cut with the cutter to the inside.

４．中心のクボミに合わせ丸い先で軽く押す。

4: Place the round end where the indentation in the center should be and lightly press.

５．彫塑べらでクボミの中心から軽く押しシワをつける。乾かす時は網の上など風通しのよい場所で乾かす。

5: Lightly press with the modeling spatula from the center to make wrinkles. When drying, place on a screen in a place with good air circulation.

６．乾いたらカッターで切り、形を整える。

6: When it is dry, trim with the cutter.

7. 240番位の紙ヤスリで粗削り
してから、600番位で仕上げる。

7: Use #240 sandpaper to sand
roughly, then finish with #600.

8. サーフェイサーを塗って目止
めする。塗らないと仕上げの塗料
が吸い込まれて、きれいに塗れな
い。

8: Apply surfacer to block the
pores. If you don't, the finishing
paint will be absorbed and will not
look good.

9. 色に合わせ缶スプレーを塗り、
仕上げはつや消しクリアーを50cm
位離しまんべんなく塗る。

9: Spray on paint to match the
color, and finish with flat clear at a
distance of 50 cm to cover.

10. 細いひも3本で玉結びする。

10: Tie a knot in three thin strings.

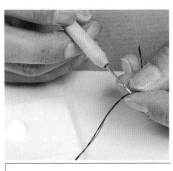

11. 木工ボンドを玉の部分につけ
る。
木工ボンドに少し水を混ぜると結
び目まで浸透しやすい。

11: Attach the knot with wood
bond. If you add a small amount
of water to the wood bond, it
enters the knot more easily.

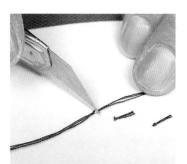

12. ボンドが乾いたら玉の中心か
ら切り、そこから5mm位の所で
切る。

12: When the bond dries, cut from
the center of the knot about 5mm
outward.

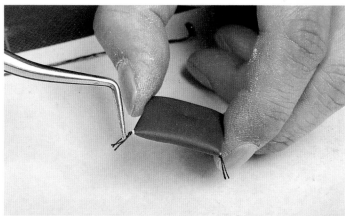

13. さらに玉の部分に木工ボンド
をつけ端に接着する。少し下向き
がよい。中心のひもは1本を1mm
の長さに切り、木工ボンドで接着
する。

13: Apply wood bond to the knot
and attach to the end. A little
downward-facing is best. Cut one
of the strings in the center to a 1-
mm length and attach with wood
bond.

14. 出来上がり。
左はスチレンペーパーを削り出し、
木工パテを塗り下地処理したもの。
右のようなくぼみがある場合はフ
ァンドを進める。木工パテはp.14-
9参照。

14: The finished model. The
zabuton on the left uses a
substrate--styrene paper shaved
down, with wood putty applied.
When you have an indentation as
on the right, clay is recommended.
For the use of wood putty see p.
14-9.

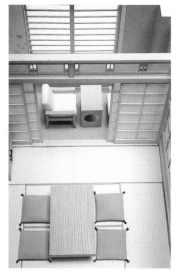

15. ホテルの内装模型。S=1/20
障子はABS板1mmを角に切り出
し、障子紙を木工ボンドで貼って
ある。畳はミューズコットンのひ
わ色を使って目に合わせて切り貼
りし、縁はパントンを細く切り貼
ってある。

15: A model of a hotel interior.
S =1/20.
The shoji are made from 1-mm ABS
board cut into squares, with the
shoji paper pasted on with wood
putty. The tatami mats use Muse
cotton cut and pasted along
the lines, with the trim made from
Pantone cut narrowly and also
pasted on.

44

カーテンの作り方 ファンドでカーテンを作ってみる。
How to Make Curtains Making curtains from clay.

◆使う物：ファンド、ベビーパウダー、彫塑べら、カッター、
紙ヤスリ、スチール定規、下敷き（ABS板など）

◆**Materials**: foundation clay, baby powder, modeling spatula, cutter, sandpaper, steel ruler, substrate (ABS board, etc.)

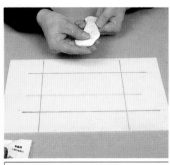

１．ABS板や厚紙にカーテンの寸法とタッセルの位置を長めの線で書いておく

1: Draw lines on ABS board or thick paper slightly longer than the dimensions necessary for the curtain and the position of the tassels.

２．カーテンの大きさに、ファンドを形に合わせる。ベビーパウダーをかけて伸ばす。

2: Shape the clay to the size of the curtain. Sprinkle on baby powder and stretch.

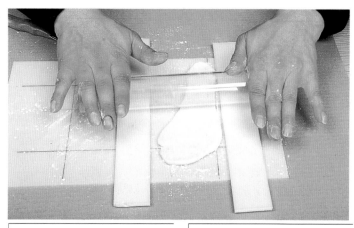

３．一定の厚みにするためには５mmスチレンなどの板を両端に置き丸パイプなどで伸ばす。丸棒などがない場合はスプレー缶などを使うとよい。

3: To make it all one thickness, place 5-mm styrene or other board at each end and stretch with a round pipe or roller. When you do not have a roller, use a spray paint can.

４．彫塑べらで押してカーテンのシワをつける。

4: Press with a modeling spatula to put wrinkles in the curtain.

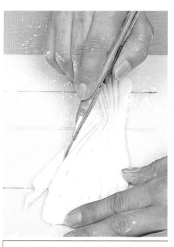

５．シワが出来たら余分な所はカッターで切り取る。

5: When the wrinkles are done, cut away the excess with the cutter.

６．乾きが早く堅くなってきたら筆で水を塗るとよい。

6: If it begins to dry too fast, moisten with a brush dipped in water.

7．タッセルの部分は、タッセルの幅に合った板（スチレンペーパー）などで両側からよせる。

7: Draw the tassels on both sides with board (styrene paper, e.g.) fit to the width of the tassels.

8．両側から絞るように寄せるとよい。上からも押してやる。

8: Draw by pressing from both sides. Also press from above.

9．この状態で固まるまで乾かす。表面が固まったら裏返しにして金網やタオルの上でさらに乾かす。左のカーテンのタッセルは手のひらでファンドを丸く伸ばし、網目をへらでつけ、タッセル部分に巻きつけた。

9: Dry like this until it hardens. When the surface becomes hard, turn it over and continue to dry on a metal screen or towel in a place with good air circulation. Here, the tassels on the left side of the curtain were stretched and rounded with the palm of the hand, and a spatula was used to score a string pattern, gathered at the top.

10．固まったら窓に合わせカッターで余分な所を切る。

10: When it hardens, line up with the window and cut the excess with the cutter.

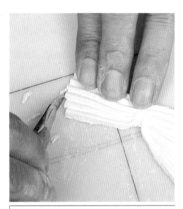

11．下の部分はこのように段差をつけて切るとよい。

11: Set the height difference at the bottom in this way and cut.

12．切り口を240番のヤスリで削る。

12: Sand the edges with #240 sandpaper.

13．紙ヤスリを丸め、溝を削る。仕上げは600番位の紙ヤスリを使う。小さなキズや穴は木工パテを見ずで溶いて埋める。

13: Roll up the sandpaper and sand the grooves. Finish with #600 sandpaper. Fill in small nicks and holes with wood putty diluted with water.

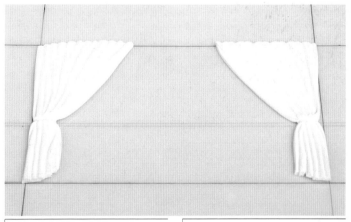

14．出来上がり。カーテンの上の部分の幅が9から比べると増えていることに気がついたと思う。乾いた後でも水をつけファンドを足すことが出来る。

14: The finished model. You might realize here that the width of the upper part of the curtain is slightly greater than in Step 9. Even after it dries, you can always put on some water and add a bit more clay.

カーテンレールの作り方 カーテンレールを作る。
How to Make a Curtain Rail Making the curtain track.

◆使う物：プラスチック棒2mmφ、丸い画鋲、ピンバエス、ペンチ、ニッパ、ABS板0.5mm、ポンチ3mmφ、真ちゅう棒0.5mmφ、アクリダイン、カッター、金の缶スプレー

◆**Materials**: foundation clay, baby powder, modeling spatula, cutter, sandpaper, steel ruler, substrate (ABS board, etc.)

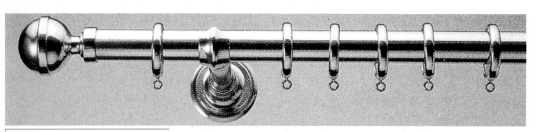

1．この商品をもとに作ってみる。

1: Let's try making this product.

2．寸法に合った丸パイプか丸棒を用意して切る。ここではプラスチック棒2mmφを使っている。切り方は、カッターの刃を乗せ、転がしながら切れ目を入れてから折る。

2: Prepare round pipe or a rod according to dimensions and cut to length. Here a plastic rod 2 mm in diameter was used. To cut, place the cutter blade on the rod, roll the rod to make a cut line and snap.

3．丸い画鋲の針の部分を3mm残しペンチで切る。

3: Cut the pin part of a round thumbtack with a cutting pliers, leaving 3 mm.

4．丸棒を使う場合はピンバエスで針を刺す穴をあける。

4: When using a rod, hold with a pin vise and push in the pin to open a hole.

6．0.5mm位の真ちゅう棒をカーテンレールより少し太めの棒に巻きつける。真ちゅうが堅くて曲がらない場合は、コンロで赤くなるまで熱してゆっくり冷ますと曲げやすくなる。真ちゅうは細かい目の紙ヤスリか磨き粉で磨いておくこと。

6: Wrap around a 0.5-mm or so brass rod that is slightly thicker than the curtain track. If the brass is too hard and does not bend, heat on a gas burner until it gets red, slowly cool and it will become easier to bend. Polish the brass using fine sandpaper or polishing powder.

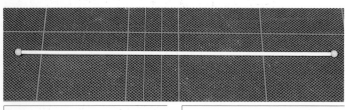

5．このようになる。接着はまだしないように。

5: It then looks like this. Do not attach yet.

7．棒から抜き、ニッパで輪になるように切る。

7: Remove from the rod and cut with the nipper to form rings.

8．レール取り付けステイを作る。ABS板か塩ビ板の0.5mmをポンチ3mm φ で抜く。

8: Make the stays to hold the curtain track. Punch out a 3-mm diameter hole in 0.5-mm ABS board or vinyl chloride board.

9．プラスチック棒をステイの長さで切る。

9: Cut plastic rod to the length of the stays.

10．丸棒をアクリダインでレールに取り付ける。後で真鍮棒を入れるので片方のみ取り付けること。

10: Attach the round rod to the rail with acridine. Do this on one side only, as later you must put in the brass rod.

12．7で切り出したリングを入れてからもう片方のステイを取り付ける。

12: Put on the rings you cut out in Step 7, then attach the other stay.

11．8で抜いた丸板を取り付ける。塩ビ板で丸板を作った場合は、エンビダインとアクリダインを混ぜ合わせて使うとよい。また、瞬間接着剤も使える。

11: Attach the round piece of board you cut out in Step 8. If you used vinyl chloride board for the piece, mix enbidine (adhesive for vinyl chloride board)) and acridine or attach with instant bond.

13．画鋲をセットしてリングを片方に寄せ、半分だけ塗装する。塗料が乾いたらリングをずらして残り半分を塗装する。リングは真鍮（金色）なので塗装する必要はない。

13: Set the thumbtack, move the rings to one side and paint half only. When the paint dries, slide the rings over and paint the other half. The rings are made of brass (gold-colored) so they do not need painting.

14．画鋲を外しリングを入れてからスチのりで固定する。

14: Remove the thumbtack, and after putting on the rings, fix in place with styrene glue.

15．ステイをスチのりで固定する。窓は透明アクリル板1mmに白い角材を貼ってある。

15: Fix the stays in place with styrene glue. The window is made from 1-mm transparent acrylic board with white square pieces pasted on.

16．出来上がり。カーテンの塗装は、下地の色を缶スプレーで塗り、薄く溶いたリキテックスを点づけして塗ってある。

16: The finished model. To paint the curtain, spray paint the base color and add dots with thinly diluted liquitex.

簡単なベッドの作り方
How to Make a Simple Bed

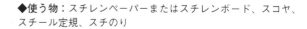

◆使う物：スチレンペーパーまたはスチレンボード、スコヤ、スチール定規、スチのり

◆Materials: styrene paper or styrene board, square, steel ruler, styrene glue

1．ダブルマットの白模型を作る。

1: Make a white model with a double mattress.

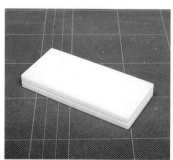

2．ベッドの幅に合わせ、スチレンボードを切り、表面の紙を剥ぐ。スチレンペーパーを使う場合はそのままで。

2: Align styrene board to the width of the bed, cut, and remove the paper backing.

3．長さに合わせてスコヤを使い、直角に2枚切り出す。

3: Align to the proper length, and using a square to make right angles, cut out two pieces.

4．コーナーを240番位の紙ヤスリで丸みをつける。2枚をスチのりで接着する。

4: Round off the corners using #240 sandpaper. Paste the two pieces together using styrene glue.

5．マット部分の出来上がり。

5: The mattress part is done.

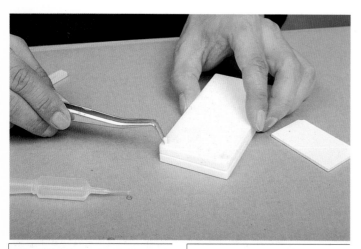

6．脚はプラスチック棒の角材を切って使うか、スチレンペーパーを角にして使う。ヘッドボードは2mmのスチレンペーパーで作る。板目を入れる時は先の尖った物で書くように跡をつける。コーナーの丸みは丸ヤスリを使う（p.102-29、30参照）。接着はスチのりで。

6: For the legs use square plastic rods or styrene paper made square. Make the headboard from 2-mm styrene paper. To put in wood grain, draw with an object with a tip to leave an impression. Use rounded sandpaper to round the corners (see p. 102-29) and attach with styrene glue.

7．出来上がり。

7: The finished model.

ベッドの作り方I
How to Make a Bed (I)

◆使う物：スタイロフォーム、ファンド、ベビーパウダー、スチール定規、スコヤ、カッター、丸棒、紙ヤスリ、ABS板2mm、アクリルカッター

◆Materials: styrofoam, foundation clay, baby powder, steel ruler, square, cutter, round rod, sandpaper, 2-mm ABS board, acrylic cutter

IN HOUSE

1．これから作るベッドの実物写真。このような布の感じを出すには、本物の布を使うことは難しい。そこでファンドを使って作ってみる。

1: A picture of the bed we are going to make. It is difficult to bring out the cloth texture using real cloth. Instead we will use foundation clay.

2．中材および型となるスタイロフォームを3枚切り出しておく。型にする2枚はスチのりで貼り合わせておく。

2: Cut out three sheets of styrofoam for the inner material and mold. Paste together two for the mold with styrene glue and let sit.

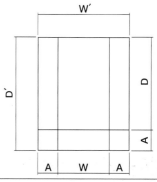

3．ファンドを切り出すためのゲージを作る。図のようにフリル部分を含めた大きさでゲージを作る。W・Dはベッドの大きさ、Aはフリル（垂れ下がり）。

3: Make a gauge for cutting the clay to size. Make the gauge according to the drawing size, including the frilled part. "W" and "D" are the bed size and "A" is the frilled hanging.

4．W′×D′の大きさにABS板をカットし、Aを記す線をアクリルカッターでV溝を入れる。

4: Cut ABS board to the size of W' and D', and cut in a V-groove with an acrylic cutter along the marked lines.

5．ファンドを6mm厚位まで指で平たく伸ばし、ベビーパウダーを両面につける。

5: Flatten and stretch the clay to a thickness of about 6-mm. Put baby powder on both sides.

6．台（ABS板か塩ビ板）にベビーパウダーをまき、ファンドを乗せ丸棒で縦と横から伸ばし、薄く広げる。2～3mm位の厚みになればよい。

6: Sprinkle baby powder on a board (ABS board or vinyl chloride board), put the clay on top and extend with a roller both horizontally and vertically. It is ready when it is about 3-mm thick.

7. もう一度パウダーをつけ、4で作ったゲージを乗せ軽く押してから、溝のある面を下にして外を切り取る。ゲージを取ればアクリルカッターでつけたV溝がくっきりと出てくる。
＊ゲージを作っておかないとファンドの切り出しや寸法出しが難しい。

7: Once more apply powder. Set the gauge that you made in Step 4 on top, press and cut away the outside (Put the side with grooves facing down). When you remove the gauge, the V-groove you notched with the acrylic cutter stands out clearly.
N.B. If you don't make a gauge, it is difficult to cut the clay and get the right dimensions.

8. ファンドについた跡に合わせ型を乗せる。

8: Place the mold on top of the impression left in the clay.

9. 指の跡を防ぐため、ベッドの大きさに合わせスチレンペーパーを切り、上に乗せる。

9: To prevent finger impressions, cut out styrene paper to the size of the bed and set on top.

10. スチール定規でコーナーに折り目をつける。

10: Put in fold lines using a steel ruler.

11. 定規の平たい部分を使い、押して折り目をはっきり出す。

11: Use the flat part of the steel ruler to press and bring out the fold lines clearly.

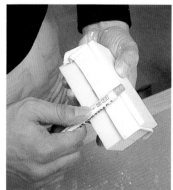

12. 丸棒で軽く押し、布のたるみの感じを出す。

12: Press lightly with a round rod to create the feel of a sag in the cloth.

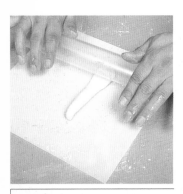

13. 枕を作る。ファンドを丸く伸ばしたあと、パウダーをつけ丸棒で平たくする。

13: Make the pillow. Round and stretch the clay, then apply powder and flatten with a roller.

14. このように中央が厚くなるように両端を薄くする。

14: In this way you make the center thick and the ends thin.

15. 枕の幅に合わせ定規で押してから、カッターで切る。

15: Line a ruler up with the width of the pillow, press, then cut.

16. ゲージに合わせ長さを切る。

16: Cut the length according to the gauge.

17. ベッドに乗せ定規で押して形を整える。この状態で1〜2日乾かす。

17: Lay on the bed and adjust the shape by pressing with the ruler. Let it dry in this state for 1-2 days.

18. 乾いたら枕カバーを取り外す。

18: When it dries, remove the pillow cover.

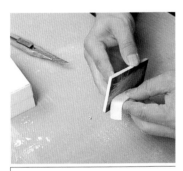

19. 240番の紙ヤスリで形を整える。

19: Adjust the shape with #240 sandpaper.

20. 600番位で丸みをつけながら仕上げる。

20: Finish with #600 sandpaper while rounding the edges.

21. ベッドの上部を平ヤスリ（ハレパネに紙ヤスリを貼った物）をかける。

21: Sand the top part of the bed with a flat file (sandpaper pasted onto adhesive styrene paper).

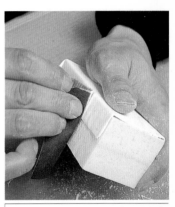

22. このような弛みは紙ヤスリを丸めてかける。

22: Round this type of sag with the sandpaper.

23. 余分な部分はカッターで切った後、ヤスリがけしておく。

23: Cut the excess parts with the cutter and sand.

24. このような溝はヤスリを折ってかけるとよい。

24: This type of groove is best sanded with folded sandpaper.

25. スタイロフォームにはめ込み、枕を乗せる。

25: Set into the styrofoam and put on the pillow.

26. ヘッドボードを作る。ABS板2mmを使い、寸法を書き入れてからアクリルカッターで木目をケガく。切り出してからケガくと持ちにくかったりケガきにくいので先にケガくように。

26: Make the headboard. Use 2-mm ABS board, draw on the dimensions and score the wood grain. If you cut it out first, it is difficult to hold and difficult to score, so do the scoring first.

27. 寸法に合わせカッターで切れ目を入れる。

27: Make enlarged cut lines according to dimensions with a cutter.

28. 折って切り出す。

28: Bend and break free.

29. コーナーをカッターで切る。このヘッドボードはp.98-1の図と同じもので作ってみる。

29: Cut the corners with a cutter. Try making this headboard exactly like the one shown in the drawing on p. 98-1.

30. 丸棒にヤスリを巻き、コーナーをヤスリがけする。

30: Wrap sandpaper around a round rod and sand the corners.

31. 平ヤスリで切り口を平らにする。

31: Sand the edges flat with the flat file.

32. サーフェイサーを塗って乾いたら軽くヤスリで仕上げ、色を吹き付ける。またはリキテックスで筆塗りする。

32: Apply surfacer, and when it dries, finish by sanding lightly, and spray from color or brush on with liquitex. If you use liquitex, it will stick better if you put on surfacer.

33. 出来上がり。ベッド部分もサーフェイサーを塗ってからプラモデル用缶スプレー3色を使い塗ってある（p.28-24参照）。仕上げはパールの缶スプレーを軽く吹き付けた。日本ペイント シルキーパール使用。

33: The finished model. For the bed part as well, surfacer was applied, then three colors of spray paint for plastic models (See p. 28-24). The finish was made with a light spray of pearl color.
• Nihon Paint's "silky pearl" was used here.

34. 写真をまねてインテリアを作ってみた。カーテンはファンドで作り、ベッドと同色に塗ってある。レースのカーテンは塩ビ板などについている保護紙をスチレンペーパーの上に乗せ、スチール定規で表と裏から強く押しジャバラ状にしてある。

34: This is an interior made to resemble the photo. The curtain is made from clay and is painted the same color as the bed. For the lace curtain, the protective paper that comes on vinyl chloride board was placed on styrene paper and a steel ruler was used to press strongly on the front and back to create accordion-like gathers.

48

ベッドの作り方II（フリル付き）
How to Make a Bed (II) (with frills)

◆使う物：スタイロフォーム、ファンド、ベビーパウダー、
スチール定規、スコヤ、カッター、丸棒、紙ヤスリ、ABS板、
真鍮棒、ハンダゴテ、ポンチ

◆Materials: styrofoam, foundation clay, baby powder, steel
ruler, square, cutter, round rod, sandpaper, ABS board, brass
bar, soldering iron, hole puncher

IN HOUSE

1. このようなフリル付きのベッ
ドカバーをファンドを使い作って
みる。

1: Let's try making this kind of bed
cover with frills from clay.

2. 「ベッドの作り方Ⅰ」と同じ工
程（2〜7）で作りコーナー部分を
切り取っておく。

2: Use the same process as for How
to Make a Bed (I), Steps 2-7, and
cut off the corners.

3. ベビーパウダーをつけ、よく
伸ばしておく。

3: Sprinkle on baby powder and
stretch.

4. ゲージの跡に合わせスタイロ
フォームを乗せる。

4: Place styrofoam on top, aligning
with the impression from the
gauge.

5. スチレンペーパーで押さえな
がら各切り口に水をつける。

5: While holding down with styrene
paper, put water on the edges.

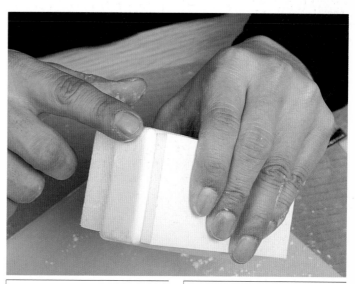

6. 切り口を寄せ合わせ指でこす
るように貼り合わせる。

6: Bring the edges together, line
them up and paste them together
by rubbing with your finger.

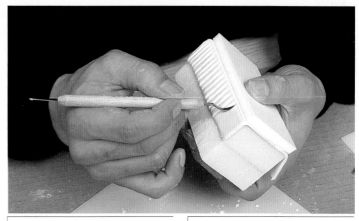

7．スチール定規でフリルの始まりを押して跡をつける。

7: Press in the beginning of the frill with a steel ruler.

8．乾き始めたら筆で水をつける。

8: When it starts to dry, brush on some water.

9．彫塑べらでフリルの溝を入れる。へらの先をフリルの始まりに合わせ押し、そのまま下げる。スベリをよくするため、へらに水をつけながらやるとよい。

9: Notch the grooves for the frills with a modeling spatula. Line up the tip of the spatula with the beginning of the frill, and press until it drops. To improve sliding, continue moistening the spatula with water.

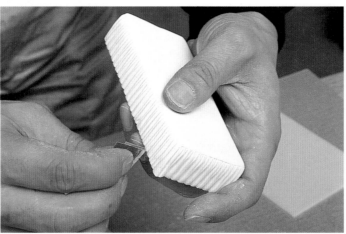

10．9でつけた溝と溝の間に先の鋭いへらで軽く押し、シワの感じを出す。出来たらこのまま1～2日乾かす。

10: Between the grooves made in Step 9, use the tip of a sharp-tipped spatula to lightly press and create a wrinkled texture. When this is done, let dry for 1-2 days.

11．完全に乾いたら型から外し、溝に紙ヤスリをかける。上下も平ヤスリをかける。

11: When it is completely dry, remove from the mold and sand the grooves with sandpaper. Sand the upper part with flat sandpaper. Then sand the bottom as well with flat sandpaper to match.

12．スタイロフォームにはめ込んで出来上がり。

12: Fit into the styrofoam and you're done.

13．出来上がり。カバーの塗装は缶スプレーの白を塗り、下の部分のレースの違いを出すために下から5mm位の所をマスキングして、もう一度白を重ね塗りした。ヘッドは真鍮棒をハンダ付けしたもの、ポールの頭はABS板を大小のポンチで抜いて作ってある。ハンダ付けは、アクリル板にABSの角材を貼りゲージを作ると簡単に出来る。

13: The finished model. The covering coat is white spray paint here. To bring out the contrast with the lace on the lower part, masking tape was applied 5 mm from the bottom, and white was painted over it. The head uses soldered-on brass rods. The head of the pole was made by punching large and small holes in ABS board. Soldering is easier if you paste square ABS board onto acrylic board to make a gauge.

14．インテリアを作ってみた。クッションはファンドで作ってある。

14: The interior. Cushions are made from foundation clay.

49

テーブルクロスの作り方

ベッドを作る方法で
テーブルクロスを作ってみる

How to Make a Tablecloth

Let's make a tablecloth using the method for making a bed

◆使う物：ファンド、ベビーパウダー、スタイロフォーム、
紙ヤスリ、スチール定規、カッター、丸棒

◆Materials: foundation clay, baby powder, styrofoam,
sandpaper, steel ruler, cutter, round rod

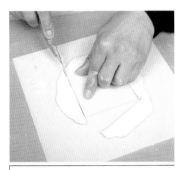

1．「ベッドの作り方Ⅰ」(p.99-2
〜6)と同じ工程で作り、ゲージに
合わせファンドをカットする。ゲー
ジは垂れる部分も入れて切り、
テーブルの大きさをアクリルカッ
ターでV溝を入れておく。

*1: Use the same process as for How
to Make a Bed (I), (p. 99, 2-6).
Align with the gauge and cut the
clay. Cut, including the part where
the gauge hangs over, and notch
a V-groove with an acrylic cutter
the size of the table.*

2．ベビーパウダーを内側になる
面にかける。
＊ゲージの線がある面を内側にす
る。

*2: Sprinkle baby powder on the
surface that will be the inside.
N.B. Put the surface that has the
gauge lines on the inside.*

3．クロスをかぶせるテーブルよ
り1mm位大きめの型をスタイロ
フォームで作り、ゲージの線に合
わせ型に乗せる。指の跡がつかな
いようにスチレンペーパーで押さ
え折り目をスチール定規で押す。

*3: Make a mold from styrofoam
about 1-mm larger than the table
the cloth will cover, and place on
the mold along the lines of the
gauge. To avoid leaving finger
impressions, hold down with
styrene paper, and press in the
fold lines with a steel ruler.*

4．1日乾かし完全に固まったら
トップは大きめの紙ヤスリをかけ
る。

*4: Dry for about one day, and
when it hardens completely, sand
the top with coarse sandpaper.*

5．側面は平ヤスリの幅を狭くし
て使うとよい。

*5: For the side it is best to narrow
the width of the flat sandpaper
before sanding.*

6．下の部分が長すぎた場合は、
鉛筆でカットラインを書く。

*6: If the bottom part is too long,
score a cut line with a pencil.*

7．線に沿って少しずつ余分な所
をカットする。

*7: Cut the excess little by little
along the line.*

8．布の弛みは、紙ヤスリを丸め
てかける。仕上げは600番位の紙
ヤスリで仕上げる。

*8: For the sag in the cloth, roll some
sandpaper and sand. Finish with
#600 sandpaper.*

9．テーブルに乗せて出来上がり。本物の布や紙では、スケールの違いで作れない。この方法だと布の弛みが容易に出来る。布に模様がある場合は、リキテックスを面相筆で描き、ツヤ消しクリヤーで仕上げる。

9: Put on the table and you are done. With real cloth or paper you cannot make the difference in scale. With this method you can make the sag of the cloth easily. If the cloth has a pattern, draw on with liquitex using a fine brush and finish with flat clear paint.

10．テーブルクロスがダブルで、下がブルー、上が白を作ってみる。ファンドのクロスに缶スプレーのブルーを塗り、乾いてからツヤ消しクリヤーを塗る。上のクロスはコピー用紙のような薄い紙にスプレーのりを吹き付ける。

10: Try making a double table-cloth, where the bottom is blue and the top is white. Spray blue onto the clay cloth and when it dries, paint with flat clear. For the top cloth, spray glue onto thin paper such as copy paper.

11．白い紙を上にかぶせて出来上がり。

11: Place white paper over it and you are done.

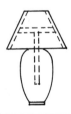

50 スタンドの作り方 ファンドを使いスタンドを作ってみる
How to Make a Lamp Stand *Using clay to make a lamp stand*

◆使う物：ファンド、丸棒、ベビーパウダー、アセテートフィルム、サークルカッター、スチール定規、カッター

◆**Materials:** foundation clay, round rod, baby powder acetate film, circle cutter, steel ruler, cutter

1．写真などから図面をおこす。カサの作り方としてはファンドで作る方法と、木型を使って熱加工で作る方法がある。ここではファンドを使った方法を紹介する。熱加工はp.25-21参照。

1: Construct a drawing from the photo. To make the shade, there are two methods--the one introduced here using clay and one using a wood formwork and heat processing. For the latter method, see p. 25-21.

2．型を作る。アセテートフィルムをサークルカッターで適当な大きさにカットする。

2: Make the form. Cut acetate film with a circle cutter to the appropriate size.

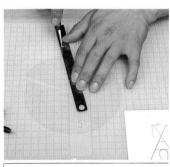

3．中心から一部切り取る。

3: Cut out a part from the center.

4．カサの角度に合わせ巻き、セロハンテープで止める。

4: Wrap around, lining up the angle of the shade and hold with cellophane tape.

5．ファンドを丸棒で2mm位の厚さに伸ばす。

5: Stretch the clay with a round rod to a thickness of about 2-mm.

6．一度型に巻き、余分な部分に印をつけカットする。

6: Wrap around the form once, mark the excess parts and cut.

7．型に巻き、切り口に水をつけ片方を上に乗せ指でよく伸ばしながらなじませる。

7: Apply water to the ends, place one side on top of the other and smooth with your finger.

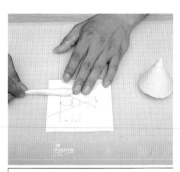

8．ツボの下地を作る。ファンドを手のひらで丸く伸ばし、形を整える。

8: Make the substrate for the stand. Round and stretch the clay with the palm of your hand to adjust the shape.

9．端にひっかけこのまま1～2日乾かす。カサは型にはめたまま半日乾かし、表面が固まったら型から外し金網のような風通しのよいものに乗せさらに乾かす。

9: Hook the edge and dry like this for 1-2 days. With the shade fit to the form, dry for half a day. When the surface dries, remove the form and place on a metal screen or other place with good air circulation to dry.

10．完全に固まったら粗目の紙ヤスリを巻き、回しながらかける。仕上げは600番の紙ヤスリを使う。

10: When it dries completely, use coarse sandpaper to sand while turning. Finish by sanding with #600 sandpaper.

11．ツボも同様に仕上げる。

11: Also, shave the stand with coarse sandpaper while turning, and finish with #600.

12．このような充電式の回転速度の遅いドリルにはさみ、紙ヤスリを巻き回転させると早くできる。

12: You can do sanding quickly by wrapping sandpaper around the drill bit of this type of rechargeable high-speed drill.

13．このように削れる。

13: Shave in this manner.

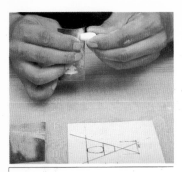

14. 糸のこで長さに合わせ切ってから切り口をヤスリがけする。

14: Cut to the proper length with a fret saw and sand the edges.

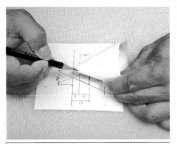

15. カサの図に合わせ印をつける。

15: Line up with the lamp shade drawing and make a mark.

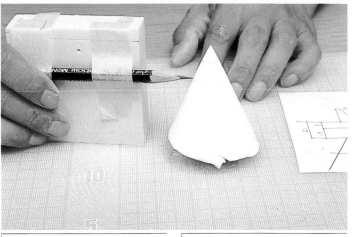

16. 印に合わせゲージを作る。型に乗せたファンドにゲージを動かし線を書く。こうすると円錐に水平に線を引くことができる。

16: Make a gauge aligned with the mark. Move the gauge to the clay that is on the mold and draw a line. In this way you can draw a level line on a cone.

17. 型から外し糸のこで線に合わせ切る。

17: Remove from the mold and cut along the line with a fret saw.

18. 上と下の切り口に平ヤスリをかける。

18: Sand the top and bottom edges using a flat file.

19. 紙ヤスリを丸めて回しながら中をかける。

19: Roll the sandpaper and sand the inside while turning.

20. ツボの中心に志棒と同寸のドリルで穴を開ける。

20: In the center of the stand, open a hole with a drill the size of the plastic rod you will use.

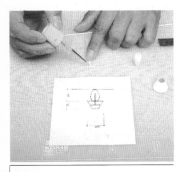

21. プラスチック棒を図のようにT形にアクリダインで接着する。

21: Attach the plastic rods together in a T-shape with acridine as shown in the drawing.

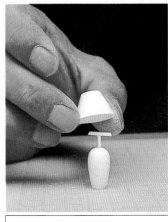

22. カサの形に合わせ斜めにカットするとカサのすわりがよい。接着はスチのりで。

22: Cut diagonally with the shape of the shade and it will line up well. Attach with styrene glue.

23. 出来上がり。ツボの塗装はリキテックスでも缶スプレーでもよい。

23: The finished model. Use either liquitex or spray paint to paint the stand.

51 洗面器の作り方
How to Make a Sink

INAX L-PG-0725

◆使う物：スチレンペーパー、スチのり、油土、石膏、紙ヤスリ、木工パテ、ようじ、カッター

◆**Materials:** styrene paper, styrene glue, oil-based clay, plaster, sandpaper, wood putty, toothpicks, cutter

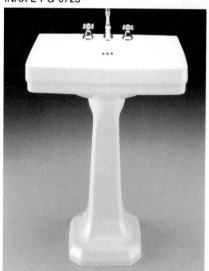

1．これから作る洗面器の実物写真。

1: This is a photo of the sink we are going to make.

2．図面をおこす。

2: Construct a drawing.

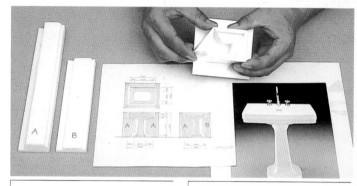

3．石膏流し込み用型枠を作る。スチレンペーパーで脚の部分をのこし型枠を作る。Aが前と左右、Bが後ろの枠材。コーナーを45°にカットしスチのりで接着し底板に固定する。

3: Make the formwork for the mold to pour the plaster into. Leave aside the leg part to be made from styrene paper. A is for the front, left and right, and B is the formwork material for the back. Cut the corners at 45-degree angles, attach with styrene glue and fix in place on the baseboard.

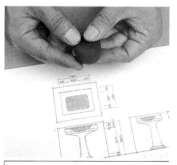

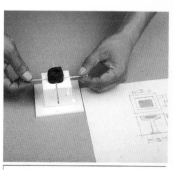

4．流しの型を作る。油土を丸くしてから指で四角にする。

4: Make the model of the sink. Round the oil-based clay and square it off with your fingers.

5．油土の型が沈まないよう深さに合わせ、ようじを刺す。埋め込む部分に中性洗剤を筆で塗っておく。離型剤の役目を果たす。

5: So that the clay doesn't sink, line up toothpicks to the right depth and push in. Apply neutral detergent with a brush to the part that will be filled in. This acts as a surface lubricant.

6．石膏を泡立てないよう溶き、型の中に流し込む。

6: Pour the plaster into the formwork without creating bubbles.

7．流しの型を前後左右の間隔を合わせ石膏の中に乗せる。

7: Place the model of the sink into the plaster, adjusting the space on the front and back, left and right.

8．40分位で型枠から外す。

8: After about 40 minutes, remove from the mold.

9．カッターで形を整える。乾いていなければカッターで容易に削ることができるが、紙ヤスリは使えない。

9: Trim the mold with a cutter. If it is not yet dry, you can easily shave with a cutter. Sandpaper, however, will not work.

10．直線的な段差は定規をあてがいカッターで軽く切れ目を入れる。

10: To make the change in levels straight, hold a ruler against it and lightly score a cut line with the cutter.

11．切れ目までカッターで削る。形が整ったらこの状態で1〜2日乾かす。

11: Shave up to the cut line with the cutter. When the mold is trimmed, let dry like this for 1-2 days.

12．完全に乾いたら240番位の紙ヤスリで粗削りする。

12: When it dries completely, sand roughly with #240 sandpaper.

13．曲面用ヤスリを作る。ハレパネに貼った紙ヤスリの裏のスチレンを4mmほど切り取り、角を押しながらRにする。

13: Make a curved file. Cut out about 4 mm of the adhesive styrene board onto which sandpaper has been stuck, and press on the corners until it bends.

14．このようにR面に合わせヤスリをかける。仕上げは600番位のヤスリで仕上げる。

14: In this way you can line up with the curved surface to sand. Finish with approximately #600 sandpaper.

15．削り過ぎやキズがある場合、木工パテを水で3：1の割合で溶き、穴やキズを埋め乾いたらヤスリがけする。

15: If you shave off too much or if there are nicks, dilute wood putty with water (3:1) and fill in the holes or nicks. When it dries, sand again.

16．出来上がり。

16: The finished model.

蛇口の作り方 プラスチック棒を伸ばして蛇口を作る
How to Make a Water Faucet *Stretching a plastic rod to make a water faucet*

◆使う物：プラスチック棒2mmφ、3mmφ、アクリダイン、木工パテ、面相筆、ライター、ABS板1mm、紙ヤスリ、ピンセット

◆Materials: 2-mm, 3-mm diameter plastic bar, acridine, wood putty, fine brush, lighter, 1-mm ABS board, sandpaper, tweezers

1．2mmφのプラスチック棒をライターでゆっくり加熱しながら柔らかくする。

1: Pass a 2-mm diameter plastic bar slowly over a lighter flame to soften.

2．熱いうちにゆっくり伸ばし細くする。

2: While it is still hot, slowly bend and make thinner.

3．伸ばしたらすばやく蛇口の曲がりに合った物に押し当て固まるのを待つ。

3: As soon as it is stretched, press against an object that matches the curve of a faucet and wait for it to harden.

4．このように出来ればよい。

4: It is good if you can make it like this.

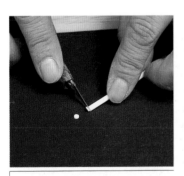

5．蛇口の下の台座を作る。3mmφのプラスチック棒を1mm位の幅にカットする。またはABS板の1mmを3mmφのポンチで抜いてもよい。

5: Make the mount for the faucet. Cut a 1 mm length of 3-mm diameter plastic rod. It is also alright to use 1-mm ABS board and punch out a hole 3 mm in diameter.

6．カットした蛇口の下にアクリダインで接着する。

6: Attach to the bottom of the faucet.

7．ハンドルを作る。1mmのABS板を1mmの幅でカットし1mmの角材を切り出し、紙ヤスリで丸くする。ハンドルを簡単に作るには2mmφのプラスチック棒をハンドルの高さでカットして作ってもそれらしくなる。

7: Make the handle. Cut a 1-mm square of 1-mm ABS board. Round with sandpaper. A simple way to make the handle is to cut 2-mm plastic rod to the height of the handle. This will also look realistic.

8．ハンドルが十になるようにパーツを切り出す。

8: Cut out the parts so that the handle forms a "+".

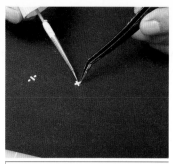

9．右のように長い物と短い物の組み合わせで十にする。ピンセットで押さえアクリダインを少しつけ接着する。固まったらたっぷりアクリダインをつけ乾かす。

9: As you see on the right, you can create a "+" by putting together a long and short pieces. Hold with tweezers, apply a tiny bit of acridine and attach. When it hardens, put on a lot of acridine and wait for it to dry.

10．小さすぎて作りずらかったら左のように長めに組み合わせてからカッターで長さに合わせ切るとよい。

10: If it is too small or has shifted, assemble a bit longer as shown on the left, then cut to the proper length with a cutter.

11．ハンドルの台座を作る。3mm φのプラスチック棒の先をカッターで細くする。

11: Make the mount for the handle. Narrow the end of 3-mm plastic rod with the cutter.

12．角を丸くしたヤスリで内側のR面を作る。

12: Using the file with rounded corners, make the inside curve.

13．台座を切る。切る寸法に合わせカッターの刃を乗せ、ころがして切る。頭にアクリダインをつけ10で作ったハンドルを中心に乗せ固定する。

13: Cut the mount. Align to the right dimensions, place the blade of the cutter on top and roll to cut. Put acridine on top, place the handle made in Step 10 and let it set.

14．ハンドルに丸みをつける。木工パテを3：1の割合で水で溶き、面相筆で先にパテを塗り丸みをつける。

14: Round the handle. Dilute wood putty well with water (3:1) and apply putty with a fine brush to the end to make it round.

15．蛇口のリングなども木工パテを一周塗り、太さを変えるとよい。

15: You can also apply wood putty to make the faucet rings or to change their size.

16．十分乾かしてからゴールドの缶スプレーで仕上げ塗りする。

16: It is good if you can make it like this. After it dries thoroughly, finish with gold spray paint.

17．スチのり（p.12-5参照）を使い接着する。

17: Use styrene glue (see p. 12-5) to attach.

18．出来上がり。

18: The finished model.

便器の作り方
How to Make a Toilet

◆使う物：石膏、スチレンペーパー、スチのり、スチール定規、カッター、木工パテ、紙ヤスリ

◆Materials: plaster, styrene paper, styrene glue, steel ruler, cutter, wood putty, sandpaper

1．この写真を基に作ってみる。

1: Make a toilet based on this photo.

TOTO CS906RG

INAX C-EL-0811475

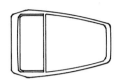
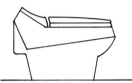

2．写真から図面をおこす。

2: Construct a drawing from the photo.

3．図面に合わせスチレンペーパーで枠を作る。フタの面に合わせ枠を一部下げている。

3: Line up styrene paper with the drawing and make the formwork. Line up the formwork with the cover and make one part lower than the rest.

4．石膏を溶き、枠に入れる。

4: Pour plaster into the formwork.

5．スチレンペーパーの切れ端を上に乗せ固める。枠の上を平らにするよりもこの方が削り出しやすいため。

5: With the cut end of the styrene paper up, place on top and let harden. Rather than making the top of the formwork flat, this way it becomes easier to shave.

6．40分位で枠から外す。

6: Wait 40 minutes and remove from the formwork.

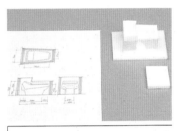

7．石膏に側面図を貼り、カッターで印をつけ切り出していく。溝になる部分もカッターで印をつける。

7: Paste the side-view drawing onto the plaster, mark with a cutter and cut out. Also mark with the cutter the part that will have a groove.

8．7で入れたカッターラインに沿ってV溝を入れる。

8: Notch a V-groove along the cut line scored in Step 7.

9．形が出来たら丸みをつけていく。この状態で1日乾かす。

9: When the mold is made, round off to reach this stage and let dry for one day.

10．完全に乾いたら240番の紙ヤスリで粗削りして600番で仕上げる。溝は紙ヤスリを折って使うとよい。

10: When it dries completely, sand roughly with #240 sandpaper and finish with #600. Sand the grooves with folded sandpaper.

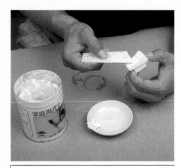

11. 穴やキズがあったら水で溶いた木工パテをへらや筆で埋め、乾いたらヤスリがけする。

11: If there are holes or nicks, fill in with diluted wood putty using a spatula or brush. When it dries, sand with sandpaper.

12. このような便器の入りずみは、リューターの先に丸刃をつけ削ると楽に削れる。

12: For the internal angle of this toilet, put a round bit into the you can more easily shave it if you apply the round blade to the tip of the router.

13. 出来上がり。サーフェイサーを2、3回塗り、完全に乾いたら600番の紙ヤスリを軽くかけてから仕上げ塗装する。塗装は缶スプレーを塗るが、サーフェイサーと同系の塗料で。

13: The finished model. For the finishing paint, apply 2 or 3 coats of surfacer, and when it dries completely, lightly sand with #600 sandpaper. Close the pores first, then paint on the finish. Use spray paint, but the same type as the surfacer.

◆使う物：型にするABS板か木材、ファンド、ベビーパウダー、カッター、紙ヤスリ

◆Materials: ABS board, foundation clay, baby powder, cutter, sandpaper

1. 便器の内側の部分をABS板や木材（バルサ）などで型を作り、ファンドにベビーパウダーをつけ型にかぶせて乾くのを待つ。

1: Use ABS board or wood (balsa) to make a form for the inside part of the urinal. Sprinkle baby powder on the foundation clay, cover the form and wait for it to dry.

2. 十分乾いたら型から外し、余分なところはカッターで形を整えてから紙ヤスリで仕上げる。型から外せない場合はかぶりがあり過ぎるのでカッターで少し切ってから外すとよい。

2: When it has dried fully, remove and cut off the excess with a cutter. After adjusting the shape in this way, sand to finish. If you have trouble removing it from the form, it means there is too much covering it, so take the cutter and cut away a bit. This should make it easy to remove.

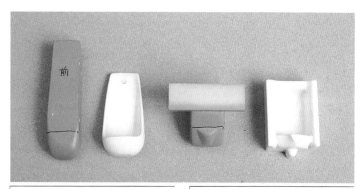

3. 型と仕上げ。このような形は石膏で作ると、外す時割れてしまうので柔軟なファンドがよい。

3: The form and the finished work. If you make this kind of form from plaster, it will break when you remove. Soft foundation clay is better.

4. 取り付け例。

4: Example of the urinal in place.

55

バスタブの作り方
How to Make a Bathtub

◆使う物：石膏、スチレンペーパー、油土、紙ヤスリ、サーフェイサー、ようじ、缶スプレー

◆**Materials:** plaster, styrene paper, oil-based clay, sandpaper, surfacer, spray paint

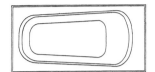

２．図面をおこす。

2: Make the drawings.

TOTO FB150S

１．実物写真。

1: Let's try making this. TOTO FB150S

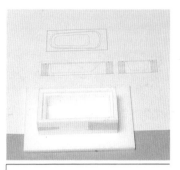

３．図面に合わせ、スチレンペーパーで枠を作る。埋め込みタイプなので、枠の内側に低いスチレンペーパーを貼り段差をつけてある。

3: Align styrene paper with the drawing and make the formwork. This is a sunk-in tub, so styrene paper is pasted low on the inside of the formwork to create the difference in height.

４．油土で型を作り、沈まないよう深さに合わせ、ようじを刺し高さを調整する。

4: Make the model from oil-based clay and so that it does not sink, stick in toothpicks at the proper depth and adjust the height.

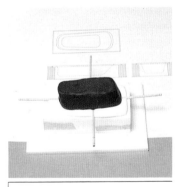

５．石膏を流し込み、型を沈める。上下左右の間隔に注意して40分位したら型と枠を外し、１〜２日乾かす。

5: Pour in the plaster, and sink in the model. Check the spaces on top, bottom, left and right, and after 40 minutes or so remove both the model and the formwork and dry for 1-2 days.

６．乾いたら紙ヤスリの240番で天板を平らにする。穴やキズがあったら木工パテを水でよく溶き、筆で埋める。

6: When it is dry, flatten the top with #240 sandpaper. If there are any holes or nicks, dilute wood putty well with water and fill in with a brush.

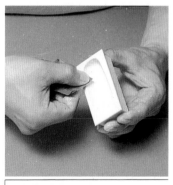

７．1000番位の紙ヤスリでコーナーに丸みをつける。

7: Round the corners with approximately #1000 sandpaper.

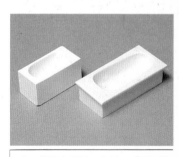

８．出来上がり。上がエプロン付きバス、下は埋め込みタイプ。

8: The finished model. Above is a bath with apron and below is the sunk-in type.

9．サーフェイサーを塗り、目を
つぶす。2回位塗り、完全に乾い
たら1000番の紙ヤスリを軽くかけ
るとツルツルになる。

*9: Apply surfacer and eliminate the
pores. Apply two times or so, and
when it dries completely, sand
lightly with #1000 sandpaper to
make it shine.*

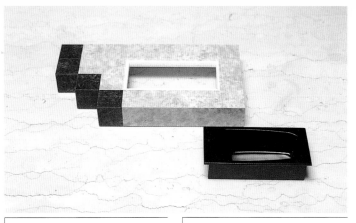

10．仕上げに缶スプレーを塗って
出来上がり。上の開口部は埋め込
み寸法で抜いて、スチレンペーパ
ーで下地を組み、大理石を貼って
ある。

*10: Use spray paint for the finish.
The open part on top is left
untouched according to the size
where the tub is to be sunk in.
Assemble the base from styrene
paper and paste on marble.*

11．この写真のイメージで浴室を
作ってみる。
TOTOのカタログより。

*11: Try making a bathroom in the
image of the one shown in this
photo.*
•From a TOTO catalog.

12．大理石を作り1～3枚で折り、
貼る。（p.37参照）

*12: Make marble. Bend 1-3 sheets
and paste (See p. 37-9).*

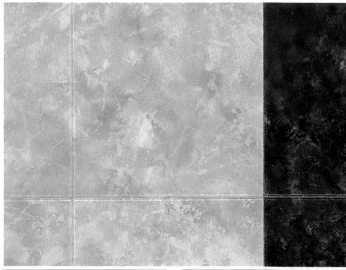

13．貼り合わせの拡大。

*13: An enlargement of the pasted
together pieces.*

14．壁のタイルはグレーのエンビ
板に白を塗りアクリルカッターで
溝を引いている。

56

ゴム型を作り量産する（片面取り）
Making a Rubber Model and Mass Producing (single-sided)

◆使う物：スチレンペーパー、スチのり、シリコン、キャスト、紙ヤスリ

◆Materials: styrene paper, styrene glue, silicon, casting agent, sandpaper

1．ソファーを型取りして量産する方法。ソファーをスチレンペーパーの上にスチのりで固定する。本体の四方および上に15mm以上の隙間をとってスチレンペーパーで枠を作る。

1: How to take a mold of a sofa and mass produce it.
Fix the sofa in place onto styrene paper with styrene glue. Allow 15 mm of space around the sides and above, and make the formwork from styrene paper.

2．大きめの容器にシリコンと硬化剤を100：5の割合で空気が入り込まないようにゆっくり混ぜる。（株）KCKシームレスシリコン使用。

2: In a large container, mix silicon and hardening agent at a ratio of 100:5, mixing slowly so that air does not get in. ●KCK seamless silicon was used here.

3．シリコンを周りからゆっくり入れる。1日おいてシリコンが固まったら枠を取り原型を外す。

3: Pour in the silicon slowly from edges. Leave for one day. When the silicon has hardened, take off the formwork and remove the model.

4．キャストA・B剤を同量ずつ紙コップで計り、混ぜ合わせゴム型一杯すれすれまで入れる。すみに泡があるときは棒ですばやく取る。プラキャストUW使用。

4: Measure equal amounts of A and B casting agent in a paper cup, mix and pour into the rubber mold until just full. If there are bubbles in the corners, remove quickly with a rod.

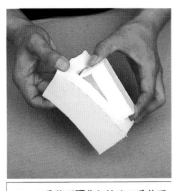

5．1分位で硬化し始め20分位で固まる。固まったらゴム型から外す。多数使用する場合はスプレー式の離型剤を使うとゴム型が長持ちする。

5: It starts hardening in one minute and takes 20 minutes to fully harden. When hard, separate from the rubber mold. If you are going to use it many times, using a spray-type surface lubricant will help the mold last longer.

6．底をヤスリで平らにする。

6: Sand the bottom flat.

7．出来上がり。同じものが幾つでも作れる。塗装する場合は、中性洗剤でよく洗い、乾いてから塗装するとよい。
＊洗わないと塗料がはがれてしまう。特に離型剤を使った場合は注意。

7: The finished work. You can make as many of the same object as you wish. If you are going to paint it, rinse thoroughly in neutral detergent and dry before painting.
N.B. If you do not rinse it, the paint will peel. This applies especially when a surface lubricant is used.

◆使う物：シリコン、油ねん土、彫塑べら、キャスト、離型剤、プラスチック棒3mmφ、ABS板かスチレンペーパー

◆Materials: silicon, oil-based clay, modeling spatula, casting agent, surface lubricant, 3-mm diameter plastic rod, ABS board or styrene paper

1．このような柱を量産する場合、2面取りしないと抜くことはできない。

1: When mass producing a column like this, a double-sided mold must be used or it will be impossible to remove.

2．まず台（ABS板）の上に油ねん土を乗せ、枠の寸法と同じ位の大きさに形を整える。柱を半分埋め込むので、柱の大きさに油ねん土を掘っておく。

2: First, place oil-based clay on the board (ABS board). Shape to about the same dimensions as the formwork. The column will be half sunk in, so dig out the clay to the size of the column.

3．油ねん土に柱を半分埋め込む。油ねん土と柱の接点の隙間をへらで埋める。

3: Half bury the column in the clay. Use a spatula to eliminate the spaces where the column and the clay contact.

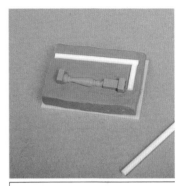

4．油ねん土を掘りプラスチック棒を半分埋め、隙間をへらで埋める。長いほうの頭が湯口（そそぎ口）になる。

4: Dig out the clay and half bury a plastic rod. Fill in the spaces with a spatula. The longer head will be used for pouring.

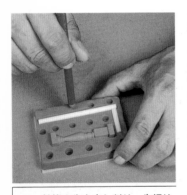

5．鉛筆の先を少し削り、先細りにして油ねん土にダボ穴をつける。

5: Scrape a bit with the tip of a pencil, taper the end and make a dimple.

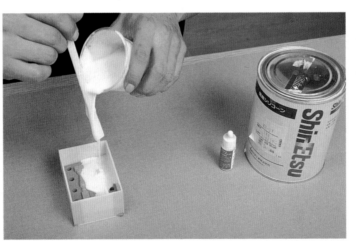

6．油ねん土にABS板で作った枠をかぶせ、テープで固定する。油ねん土と枠との隙間もへらで埋めておく。シリコンを容器に取り、硬化剤を入れゆっくりとよく混ぜ、容器からシリコンを少しずつ流し込み、型（柱）のトップから10mm以上になるように入れる。シリコンは信越シリコーンRTVゴム使用。

6: Cover the clay with the formwork made of ABS board and fix in place with tape. Fill the spaces between the clay and the formwork using a spatula. Put silicon in a container, add hardening agent and slowly mix. Little by little pour the silicon into the formwork, from 10-mm or more above the top of the model (column). The silicon used here was Shin'etsu silicon RTV rubber.

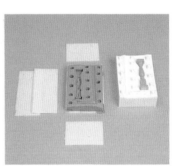

7．硬化したら枠を外す。このように油ねん土部分と別れる。ダボ穴がシリコン側では凸になっている。

7: When it hardens, remove the formwork. In this way separate it from the clay part. The dimple sticks out on the silicon side.

8．ABS板の枠をシリコン型に巻きテープで固定する。油ねん土と違いゴムどうしだとついてしまうので離型剤（バリヤコート）を筆でシリコンゴムに塗る。

8: Wrap the ABS board formwork around the silicon model and fix in place with tape. Unlike with clay, since these are both rubber materials, they will stick, so brush a surface lubricant (barrier coat) onto the silicon rubber.

9．シリコンゴムを注ぐ。

9: Pour the silicon rubber.

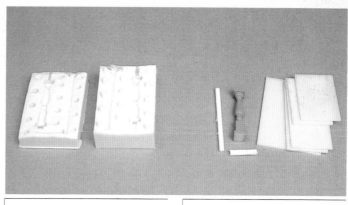

10．硬化したら枠を外し型を割る。バリヤコートの膜が残っているのでセロハンテープをつけながら取る。赤く塗ってある上の左右が湯口と空気抜き穴になる部分。下の赤い部分は通り道になるのでここも後で切る。

10: When it hardens, remove the formwork and separate the molds. A film of barrier coat remains, so remove by sticking on cellophane tape. The upper left and right painted red is the pouring end and the part with the air vent hole. The red part below is just to help the flow, so it will also be cut later.

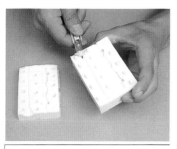

11．赤く塗った部分を切る。できるだけ2つを合わせたとき円錐形になるように切る。この部分は注ぎ口になるので入り口部分を大きくする。柱の頭は空気抜き。

11: Cut the parts painted red. As much as possible align the two and cut to form a conical shape (This part is the pouring end, so make the opening large). The top of the column is the air vent.

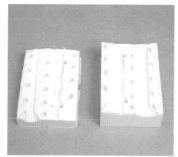

12．割り型の完成。5でつけた穴がこのように凹凸になる。これは型のずれを防ぐため。

12: The completed split model. The hole you made in Step 5 creates these indentations and projections. This is to prevent the model from sliding.

13．キャストを注入する。割り型を輪ゴムで止め、A剤とB剤を同量容器に入れ素早く混ぜ、湯口（注ぎ口）から注ぐ。空気抜きからキャストがあふれたら止める。キャストはプラキャストのベージュ使用。

13: Inject the casting agent. Hold the split mold with a rubber band. Put equal amounts of the A and B agents in a container and mix quickly, pour in through the pouring end (injection opening). When the casting agent overflows through the air vent, stop pouring. The casting agent used here is beige plastic casting agent. There is also white.

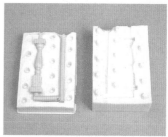

14．10分から20分で硬化したら型を外す。

14: After it hardens in 10-20 minutes, remove the form.

15．ニッパで余分な所を切る。気泡が入り穴が出来てしまったら、A剤とB剤を少量混ぜ固まり始めたら、細い棒で取り穴を埋める。

15: Cut the excess with the nipper. If air bubble entered and holes were made, mix a small amount of A and B agents, and when it starts to harden, scoop with a narrow rod and fill the holes.

16．出来上がり。

16: The finished work.

17．この柱を使ったインテリア。柱の上の壁はスチレンペーパーに木工パテ処理した後リキテックスをティッシュペーパーで塗ってある。床はABS板にグリッドを入れてから直接缶スプレーで塗り、マスキングしてラインを塗り、仕上げにクリヤーで光沢を出している。照明は熱加工（p.25-21参照）で作る。

17: An interior made with the column. The wall above the column is made of styrene paper processed with wood putty, painted with liquitex using a tissue. The floor is ABS board with a grid scored, sprayed directly with spray paint, and finished with lines painted using masking tape and a clear paint to bring out the luster. The lights were made by adding heat (See p. 25-21).

◆使う物：アクリル板、マスキングシート、スチール定規、
カッター、ツヤ消しクリヤー

◆Materials: acrylic board, masking sheet, steel ruler, cutter,
flat clear paint

1．透明アクリル板1mmを用意し、全体的にマスキングシートを貼り、透明にしたい部分に線を書き、その線に沿ってカッターで軽く切れ目を入れる。

1: Prepare 1-mm transparent acrylic board (Vinyl chloride board is okay, but it is not transparent enough). First put a masking sheet over the entire board, draw a line for the part you want to make transparent, and lightly draw the cutter along that line.

2．透明にしたい部分だけを残して、マスキングシートを全部はがす。

2: Leave just the part that you want to be transparent, and peel off all the rest of the masking sheet.

3．ツヤ消しクリヤーを塗る。一度乾かしてからもう一度遠くの方から左右に振りながら霧を落とすような感じで、少しかけては乾かし、またかける。それを2、3度繰り返すとよい。
＊スプレーは前もってぬるま湯で温めておくと粒が細かく出て本物らしくなる。

3: Next, paint on flat clear paint. When it dries, spray on again from farther away, in a swinging motion left and right to lay on a mist. Do a bit, let dry, and spray more. Repeat this two or three times.
N.B. Warm the spray can ahead of time by placing it in hot water. This way, the drops come out very fine and the finish looks realistic.

5．出来上がり。

5: The finished work.

4．乾いたらマスキングシートをはがす。はがした所だけ透明になる。

4: When it dries, peel off the masking sheet. Only that part remains clear.

タペストリーガラスの作り方
缶スプレーを直接吹く方法と
コンプレッサーを使って吹く方法

How to Make Tapestry Glass
*Two methods of making tapestry glass:
direct spraying from a can and using an air brush*

◆使う物：ツヤ消しクリヤー、クリヤーブルー、クリヤーイエロー、紙コップ

◆Materials: flat clear paint, clear blue, clear yellow, paper cup

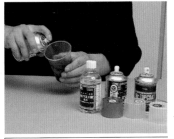

1．ツヤ消しクリヤー、クリヤーブルー、クリヤーイエローを使いタペストリー風に作ってみる。まず透明板にツヤ消しクリヤーを塗る。乾いたらクリヤーブルーをぬるま湯で温めてから50cm位上から振りながらかぶせるように少し塗る。次にクリヤーイエローを同じように塗る。塗り過ぎないように少しずつ塗り色を合わせる。

1: Let's try making a model of tapestry glass using flat clear, clear blue, and clear yellow. First, paint a transparent board with flat clear using the method described above. When it dries, warm clear blue in hot water and spray a little on from a distance of 50 cm or so above the board in a swinging motion to cover. Next, paint clear yellow in the same way. Paint little by little being careful not to overpaint, in order to adjust the color.

2．コンプレッサーがある場合は、ツヤ消しクリヤーを紙コップに吹き付け取り出し、クリヤーブルーとイエローを少し吹き付け色を合わせ、薄め液を入れよく混ぜる。

2: When you have an air brush, spray flat clear into a paper cup, remove, spray a little clear blue and yellow, put in thinner and mix.

3．ハンドピースに移し、吹き付け乾いたらもう一度塗る。好みの色（ツヤ消し）になるまで重ね塗りしたりブルーまたはイエローを足したりする。乾くとくもりの具合が変わるので注意。

*3: Pour back into the air brush, spray onto the board, and when it dries, paint again. Continue layering, adding blue and yellow until it reaches the desired color (flat).
N.B. When it dries, the cloudiness changes.*

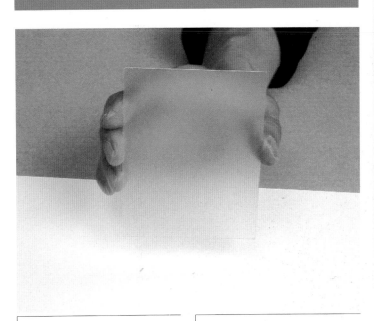

4．出来上がり。

4: The finished work.

5．渋谷BEEMの模型。中に照明を入れて夜のタペストリーガラスの効果を出している。

5: A model of Shibuya BEEM. A light was put inside to bring out the effect of the tapestry glass at night.

60 面とりガラスの作り方
How to Make Beveled Glass

◆使う物：クリヤー、クリヤーブルー、クリヤーイエロー、
透明アクリル板0.5mm、マスキングテープ、カッター、コン
プレッサー

◆Materials: glossy clear, clear blue, clear yellow, 0.5-mm
transparent acrylic board, masking tape, cutter, air brush

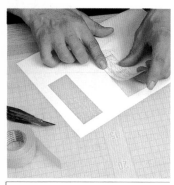

１．0.5mmの透明アクリル板にマ
スキングシートかテープを貼って
おき、図面をコピーし裏からスプ
レーのりをかけて貼り合わせる。

1: Cover 0.5-mm transparent
board with masking sheet or tape,
copy the drawing, spray on glue
from the back and paste on.

２．カッターで面とり部分をカッ
トする。

2: Cut the beveled part with the
cutter.

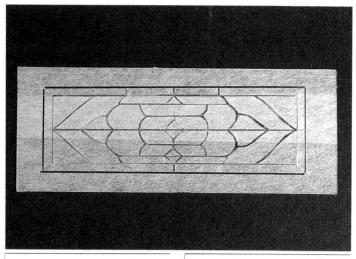

３．図面を取り、面とり部分のマ
スキングをはがす。

3: Remove the drawing and peel
off the masking on the beveled
part.

４．クリヤーとクリヤーブルー、
クリヤーイエローを量に注意しな
がら薄め液で混ぜ、ハンドピース
で吹き付ける。一度乾かしてから
もう一度塗る。ここではツヤのあ
るクリヤーを使う。

4: Mix glossy clear, clear blue and
clear yellow with thinner, and
spray on with an air brush. Let it dry
and spray again.
N.B. This time you are using glossy
clear. Color adheres with only a
little blue and yellow. Don't put in
too much.

５．出来上がり。缶スプレーで直
接クリヤーを塗り、少しクリヤー
ブルーとクリヤーイエローを吹き
付けても出来る。

5: The finished work. It is also okay
to spray directly from the can. See
the previous page (59-1). Only this
time you are using glossy clear.

61

ガラス風に仕上げる方法
アクリル板の切り口を塗って
ガラス風に仕上げる

How to Make a Glass-like Finish
Paint the cut edge of the acrylic board and finish to resemble glass

◆使う物：透明アクリル板、クリヤー、クリヤーブルー、クリヤーイエロー、薄め液、筆

◆Materials: glossy clear, clear blue, clear yellow, thinner, brush

１．p.122 の面とりガラスと同じ塗料でアクリル板の切り口のみを筆で塗る。

1: Paint in the same way as with beveled glass (p.122), and paint only the edge of the acrylic board with a brush.

２．はみ出た所は、薄め液をしみ込ませたティッシュペーパーで拭き取る。

2: Wipe the part that sticks out with a tissue soaked in thinner.

３．左はアクリル板をそのまま、右はガラス風に仕上げたアクリル板。

3: On the left is plain acrylic board. On the right is acrylic board with a glass-like finish.

62

丸柱（エンタシス）の作り方
How to Make a Round Column (Entasis)

◆使う物：スタイロフォーム、ヒートカッター、カッター、スチレンペーパー 3mm、円定規、紙ヤスリ

◆Materials: styrofoam, 3-mm styrene paper, sandpaper

１．ヒートカッターでスタイロフォームを真四角に切る。ここでは一番太い部分が19mmφなので20mm厚のスタイロフォームを20mmの幅で切った。

1: Cut the styrofoam into a perfect rectangular block using a heat cutter. The thickest part here has a diameter of 19 mm, so the styrofoam was cut to a 20-mm width.

２．円定規で付け根の部分の太さをサインペンで書く。ここでは16mmφにしてある。端の16mmφに合わせカッターで切る。1mmほど大きめにしておくこと。

2: Use a circular template to draw a circle with a felt-tip pen for the end of the pillar. Here the diameter is 16 mm.Line up the cutter with the 16-mm diameter end and cut with the cutter, 1 mm larger all around.

３．240 番の紙ヤスリで粗削りして丸みを整える。

3: Use #240 sandpaper to sand roughly and round the shape.

４．紙ヤスリを巻き回しかける。この時点で端を16mmφに合わせる。

4: Wrap the sandpaper around and sand. At this time·make sure the ends are 16-mm in diameter.

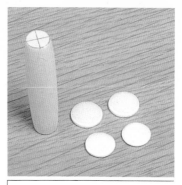

5．台座を作る。3mm厚のスチレンペーパーに台座の大きさ20mm φと24mm φを書き、カッターで少しずつカットして円に切り出す。ポンチがある場合は、ポンチでスチレンペーパーを抜けばきれいにできる。

5: Make the pedestal. Draw 20-mm and 24-mm diameter circles on 3-mm styrene paper and cut out little by little with the cutter. If you have a hole puncher, the circles will come out cleaner if you can punch through the styrene paper.

6．600番の紙ヤスリで角を丸くする。

6: Round off the corners using #600 sandpaper.

7．パーツの出来上がり。

7: The parts are completed.

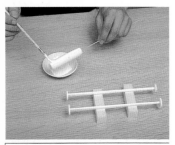

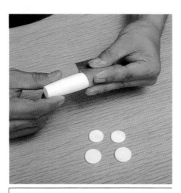

8．スタイロフォームのままでは、仕上げがきれいにならないので、スタイロフォームの目を埋めるために木工パテを3：1の割合で水で溶き筆で塗る。早く乾かしたい時はドライヤーを遠くから当てる。乾いたら600番の紙ヤスリで仕上げる。

8: The finish on plain styrofoam does not look nice, so to fill in the pores, brush on wood putty diluted in water (3 parts putty to 1 part water). When you want it to dry quickly, use a dryer from a distance. When it dries, sand with #600.

9．紙ヤスリを巻き、柱を回してかけるとよい。2、3回パテを塗りヤスリがけするとツルツルになる。

9: Wrap the sandpaper around the column and sand. Apply wood putty two or three times and sand to make it shine.

10．出来上がり。

10: The finished work.

11．パテのままだと水性塗料を塗るとパテが溶けてしまうので、プラモデル用サーフェイサーで目止めする。Mr.ホワイトサーフェイサー使用。
＊ラッカー系のサーフェイサーや塗料を塗ると下地のスタイロフォームが溶けてしまうので注意。

11: Apply surfacer. With only putty on the surface, the putty will dissolve if you apply a water-based paint, so cover with surfacer for plastic models.
N.B. Do not use lacquer-based surfacer or paint, or else the styrofoam substrate will melt.

12．塗装してインテリアの一部を作ってみた。大理石塗装はp.35-7参照。

12: After painting, a part of the interior was made. For the use of marble paint, see p. 35-7.

63

樹木の作り方 ケヤキ風の立ち木を作ってみる
How to Make a Standing Tree *Let's try making a tree that looks like a zelkova (keyaki)*

◆使う物：電気コード、ハンダ、ニッパ、缶スプレー、木工ボンド、グランドフォーム、マスプランティングシート

◆Materials: electrical cord, solder, nipper, spray paint, wood bond, groundfoam, masplanting seet

1．電気コードのビニールをカッターで縦に裂き、銅線を抜き出す。これが木の幹になる。ここで作る木の高さは6cmだが2cmほど長く切っておく。

1: Use a cutter to slice open the rubber covering of an electrical cord length-wise. Take out the copper wire. The wire will be used for the tree trunk. The height of the tree will be 6-cm here, but cut about 2-cm longer.

2．幹を太くしたいので同じものをもう1本足して、これを根元で回して1本に束ねる。

2: You want to make the trunk thick, so add another piece of wire. Twist together at the roots to bundle into one tree.

3．根元から2cm位のところをハンダ付けする。「ステンレス用フラックス」を使うとつきがよい。最後に中性洗剤で洗ってフラックスを落としておく。

3: Solder about 2-cm up from the roots. It will hold together better if you use flux for stainless steel. Finally, rinse with neutral detergent to remove the flux.

4．根元から順に枝を作っていく。まず数本に分けてねじり、枝分かれさせ幹を2、3回ねじる。また数本をねじり枝分かれさせる。

4: Make branches, starting from the bottom. First, separate several strands of wire, and twist into a branch. Twist the trunk two or three times. Again twist a few strands into a branch.

5．同様に上の方まで枝分かれさせたら、枝をさらに細かく分け、先の方までさらに分ける。ねじりながらケヤキらしい枝振りに整える。

5: You make branches in this way from bottom to top, further separating each branch down to the tip. By continuing to twist, you can shape the branches to look very much like zelkova.

6．先が長すぎるところはニッパで切る。

6: Where the ends are too long, you can cut with the nipper.

7．適当な台（スチレンボードなど）に差し込み、グレーの缶スプレーを満遍なくかける。次に茶色の缶スプレーを40cm位離して軽く押し、ツブ状に吹き付ける。

7: Insert into some kind of mount (styrene board, for example) and spray entirely with gray paint. Next, spray with brown at a distance of about 40-cm, pressing lightly to spray on drops.

8．台から抜き、枝全体に木工ボンドをたっぷり塗る。

8: Remove from the mount and apply lots of wood putty all over the branches.

9．上からジオラマ用のグランドフォームを振りかける。次に逆さまにして同じようにかける。パウダーが少なかったり、モッコリした感じにしたければ、乾かしてからさらにボンドをつけパウダーをかければよい。

9: From above sprinkle wood powder used in dioramas. Next, turn upside down and sprinkle in the same way. If the powder layer is too thin or you want it to be fuller, let it dry then add bond and sprinkle more powder.

10．出来上がり。

10: The finished model.

11．マスプランティングシートを使って垣根を作ってみる。頭を三角形にハサミで切り木工ボンドを水で少し薄め、筆で塗りグランドフォームをふりかける。左下は厚めのマスプランティングシートに塗装した真鍮棒を木工ボンドでさしてハサミで形を作りグランドフォームをつける。

11: To make a fence with a length of Massplanting sheet, cut the top of the sheet with scissors, apply diluted wood bond with a brush, and sprinkle Groundfoam over it. To make a fence like the one shown in the photo on the left, use wood bond to attach a painted stainless steel bar to a length of thick Massplanting sheet, cut the sheet with scissors, and sprinkle it with Groundfoam.

鉢植えのベンジャミンの作り方

How to Make a Potted Benjamin Tree *The Benjamin tree as an indoor potted plant*

64

◆**使う物**：真鍮棒、缶スプレー、木工ボンド、糸のこ、カッター、ファンド

◆**Materials:** brass rod, spray paint, wood bond, fret saw, cutter, foundation clay

１．幹にする適当な長さの真鍮棒を３本用意する。この３本を１本により、グレーと茶の缶スプレーをかける。

1: Prepare three brass rods of a suitable length for the trunk. Twist the three into one and spray gray and brown.

２．長さ５cm位で切り、先を三つ又に広げ木工ボンドをたっぷりつける。

2: Cut to a length of about 5 cm, and spread the end into three. Put a lot of wood bond on this part to form a ball.

３．ツブの大きなパウダーをつける。

3: Sprinkle on coarse-grained powder.

４．乾いたら上からボンドをつける。

4: When it dries, apply bond from above.

5．ツブの細かいパウダーをつけ、大きくして出来上がり。

5: Sprinkle on fine-grained powder, enlarging the top and you're done.

6．鉢を作る。パイプを糸のこで適当な長さにカットする。その他の方法として熱加工で作る方法（p.25-21参照）とファンドで作る方法がある。

6: Make the pot. Cut pipe to a suitable length with a fret saw. You can also use a heat processing method (see p. 25-21) or make it from foundation clay.

7．鉢の上になる内側はカッターで削って薄くする。底は外側にヤスリをかけて丸くする。塗装は缶スプレーでもリキテックスでもよい。

7: Shave thin the upper inside of the pot with the cutter. Round the bottom by filing down the outside. For paint, either spray paint or liquitex is okay.

8．中に粘土やファンドなどをつめる。その上から木工ボンドをつける。

8: Fill with clay. Apply wood bond on top.

9．さらに上から土のパウダーをかける。

9: Then sprinkle ground powder from above.

10．粘土が乾かないうちにベンジャミンの幹を差し込んだら出来上がり。

10: Before the clay dries, insert the trunk of the Benjamin tree and the model is complete.

11．ツボと鉢植え。左のツボはファンドを丸く形を整え、1日乾かし表面が固まったら口の部分をカットする。中はまだ固まっていないので耳かきでファンドをかきとるとツボが出来る。

11: Pot and potted plant. To make the pot on the left, form foundation clay into a round shape and let dry for one day. When the surface becomes hard, cut the mouth. The inside is not dry yet, so scoop out the clay with an ear scoop to finish the pot.

65 並木と道の作り方 芝生と立ち木を両側にあしらった道路
How to Make a Row of Trees and Road A road with lawn and trees on both sides

◆使う物：スチレンペーパーかABS板、木工ボンド、シーナリパウダー、マスキングテープ、缶スプレー（グレー、白、ダークグレー）、粘着テープ、カッター、中性洗剤、スポイト、ハケ

◆Materials: styrene paper or ABS board, wood bond, scenery powder, masking tape, spray paint (gray, white, dark blue), adhesive tape, cutter, neutral detergent, eye dropper, brush

1．下地はアクリル板、ABS板、スチレンペーパーなど水で濡れても反らない材料を用意する。道路と歩道になる部分を残して後はマスキングする。大きな面は紙などを使ってマスキングする。

1: For the substrate use acrylic board, ABS board or styrene paper--a material that will not bend when it gets wet. Mask everything except the road and sidewalk. Use paper or other material to mask the large surface.

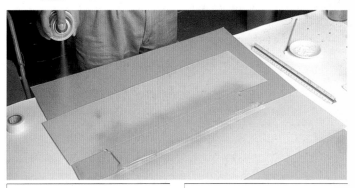

2．道の色を塗る。歩道も含め道の色を塗る。2度塗りは50cm位離して塗りツヤを消す。またはツヤ消しクリヤーを塗る。スチレンペーパーを使うときはプラモデル用缶スプレーか水性系缶スプレーを使うこと。

2: Apply color to the road. Paint the road and sidewalk together. The second coat should be from a distance of 50 cm or so using flat paint or flat clear. When using styrene paper, use surfacer for plastic models or water-based spray paint.

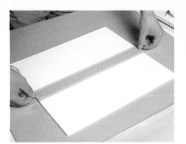

3．歩道を塗る。乾いたら歩道を残して道路だけをマスキングする。

3: Paint the sidewalk. When it dries, leave the sidewalk and mask just the road.

4．コンクリート風に仕上げてみる。まずグレーの缶スプレーで基本色を塗る。次に白とダークグレーをツブツブに塗る（p.38-10 参照）。乾いたらマスキングを全部はがす。

4: Paint the sidewalk. Try finishing the sidewalk to look like concrete. First, spray on gray as a base color. Next, paint white and dark gray to make it grainy (See p. 38-10). When it dries, remove the mask-ing from the entire board.

5．道にセンターラインを貼る。粘着テープ「アイシーテープ」か「レトラテープ」を貼る。カッターで切れ目を入れてテープを等間隔にはがす。

5: Paste a center line onto the road using the adhesive line tape "IC tape" or "Letra-tape". Score cut lines with the cutter, and peel off the tape at equal intervals.

6．横断歩道を作る。やや太めの粘着テープを貼り、カッターで切って作っていく。

6: Make the crosswalk. Stick on wide adhesive tape and cut with the cutter to create.

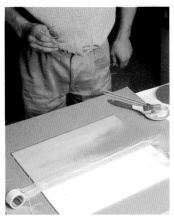

7．芝生を作る。まず歩道と道路をマスキングテープでマスキングする。木工ボンドに緑の水性絵の具と水を少量加え、大きめのハケでむらなく塗る。ボンドに色を入れたのは下地の白を見えにくくするため。

7: Make the grass. First, mask the sidewalk and road with masking tape. Add green watercolor paint and a little water to wood bond and paint thoroughly with a big brush. The reason white is added to the bond is to make the white underlay more difficult to see.

8．芝生用シーナリパウダーを振りかける。全体的にかけ終わったら息を吹きかけ余分なパウダーをはらう。そのままにしておくと余分なパウダーにボンドが吸い寄せられデコボコになってしまうので注意。茶コシにパウダーを入れて振ると均等にかけられる。

8: Sprinkle on scenery powder used for green grass. Sprinkle over the entire board and when you are done, blow off the excess powder. If left as is, the extra powder absorbs the bond and lumps form. If you put the powder in a tea strainer and shake, it gets distributed evenly.

9．出来上がり。下地が見えるようであれば2度塗りする。2度目はパウダーが乾いたら木工ボンド1に対し水を3と中性洗剤を数滴入れ、スポイトかハケでたらすと浸透性がよくなり一定に塗れる。その後パウダーを振りかけすぐに余分なパウダーをはらう。

9: The finished model. If you can see the underlay, paint a second time. This time, when the powder dries, add a few drops of neutral detergent to the wood bond (1 part bond to 3 parts water) and drop on with an eye dropper or big brush. This will improve permeation to help paint evenly. Then sprinkle on the powder and immediately blow away the excess powder.

10．前に作ったケヤキ風の立ち木を道沿いに植えてみた。根元の緑はツツジに見立てたもの。グランドフォームをボンドで接着してある。

10: Here we "planted" the zelkova tree that we made before on the roadside. The green around the roots are made to look like azalea bushes. Large-grained powder was stuck on with bond.

作 品 名：「カルテ」（化粧品）
　　　　　百貨店インショップデザイン
企画制作：株式会社官浪商品環境研究所
撮 影 者：金沢　靖

Piece name: "Carte" (cosmetics) department store in-shop design
Planning and production: Miyanami Product Research Institute
Photographer: Yasushi Kanazawa

S＝1/30 のショップモデル。本体
はABS板にラッカー塗装。壁面の
四角のボックスは透明アクリル板
3mmを四角にカットし、前面のガ
ラス部分をマスキングしてグレー
の缶スプレーを吹き付け、次にピン
クを塗ってある。マスキングを
はがせば、中がグレーのガラスの
ボックスができる。文字はインレ
タ（クロマテック）を使い、本物
らしく演出してある。

This is a shop model.(S=1/30) The
main body is made of ABS board
painted with lacquer. The walls
forming a box are made from 3-
mm acrylic board cut into squares.
The glass parts are masked off,
sprayed first with gray paint, then
pink. When the masking tape is
removed, inside it forms a gray
glass fan-shaped box. Instant
lettering was used for the lettering
to make it realistic-looking.

和食レストランの模型。S＝1/30

A model of a Japanese restaurant. (S=1/30)

本体はスチレンペーパーに色紙を貼ってある。床はABS板にアクリルカッターで溝を彫り、リキテックスで着色。畳は紙（ミューズコットンひわ色）にICテープの黒を着色し貼ってある。柱はヒノキの角材を着色し貼ってある。瓦はABS板3mmに溝を入れ作った。ロゴはインレタで作ってある。

The main body is made of styrene paper with colored paper pasted onto it. The floor is made of ABS board with a groove cut in using an acrylic cutter and colored using liquitex. The tatami mats are made of paper (Muse cotton "hiwa" light green) with the black lines made of IC tape. The pillars are made of "hinoki" wood material that is colored and pasted on. The tiles are made of 3-mm ABS board with grooves cut in. The logo is done with instant lettering.

飲食店の模型。S＝1/30

Restaurant model (S=1/30)

中央の石張りのジャモンは、黒い
ツヤのある紙にティッシュペーパ
ーでグリーンの色を塗った物をカ
ットして貼ってある（p.42-14 参
照）。柱は黒く塗ってから面相筆で
石風に仕上げてある。テーブルは
0.5mmのアクリル板を石風に加工
しカットした。カウンターはABS
板1mmを加工、フローリングは
ABS板にアクリルカッターで溝を
入れ塗装してある。

This is a model of a restaurant. The serpentine decorative stone in the center is made from black glossy paper cut up and pasted on that is colored with green rubbed on using a tissue (See p. 42-14). The pillars are painted black and then decorated using a fine brush to make it look like stone. The tables are made of 0.5-mm acrylic board processed to look like stone and cut. The counter is made of processed 1-mm ABS board and the flooring is ABS board with a groove cut in using an acrylic cutter, then painted.

Elegance Cosmetics 店舗展開プラン：パターン 1 （S＝1/10）
Elegance Cosmetics store display plan: Pattern 1 (S=1/10)

本体はABS板1mmで組み立ててある。ボトルはABS板を削り出し、塗装してある。スリガラスはツヤ消しクリヤーを塗ってある。ファンデーションはポンチで色紙を抜いて貼ってある。コーナーのゴールドはカッティングシートを細く切り貼ってある。

The main body is made of assembled 1-mm ABS board. The bottle was made by shaving ABS board and painting it. The frosted glass is made with clear matte spray paint. The foundation is made by pasting on round spots of colored paper cut out using a hole puncher. The gold on the corners is made by cutting a cutting sheet thinly and pasting on.

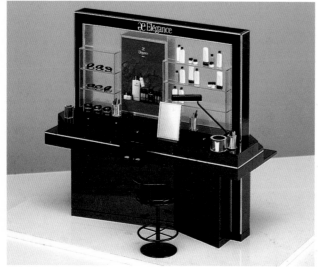

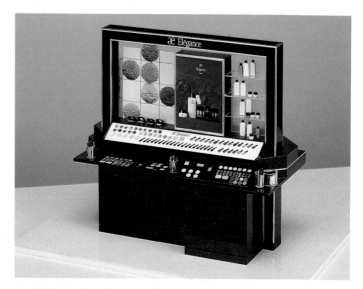

パターン 2 （S＝1/10）
Pattern 2 (S=1/10)

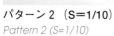

駅前開発プレゼン模型

Toke Station-front Development Presentation Model

床はABS板にアクリルカッターで目地を入れてからマスキングで色分けしてある。建物はスチレンペーパーの下地に色紙を貼ってある。

The floor is ABS board with joints cut in using an acrylic cutter. Different parts are colored with the use of masking tape. The building is made of a styrene paper underlay with colored paper pasted on.

東急ハーヴェストクラブ鬼怒川（S＝1/300）
撮影：小野達夫
東急ハーヴェストクラブ鬼怒川、SPAX鬼怒川

Tokyu Resort S=1/300
Photography: Tatsuo Ono
Tokyu Harvest Club Kinugawa, SPAX Kinugawa

川は本物の小石を使い、川底に敷き透明アクリル板2mmの裏からクリヤーブルーを塗ったものをかぶせる。その板のうえにスタイロフォーム20mmを重ね貼りして木工パテと石膏を混ぜたもの（p.15-10参照）で岩風に下地を作り、紙粘土で形を整える。塗装は筆とティッシュペーパーで塗ってある。

The river employs real pebbles laid along the bottom, covered by transparent 2-mm acrylic board painted clear blue on the reverse side. 20-mm styrofoam is pasted on top of this board, and a stone-like underlay is created using a mixture of wood putty and plaster (see p. 15-10) formed to shape with paper clay. Painting is done with brush and tissue.

まだ私の頭の中にしかない3次元の世界を第三者に理解してもらうために、計画の各段階においてモデルを製作することは、私にとって最も有効な手段である。

そして倉林氏はある時は一枚の簡単なスケッチから、またある時は基本設計図から、そしてまたある時は詳細な実施設計図から私の表現したいことを適切に読み取り、効果的なモデルを作ってくれるプレゼンにはかかせない人であり、また十数年来の悪友でもある。

下の写真は浜野商品研究所在職中担当した21ヘクタールにもおよぶウォーターフロント開発のマスタープラン時のモデルである。21世紀に実現するであろう高層ビルの林立する街の全体像を地域住民に、地権者に、そしてこれからビルを計画していくであろう多くの人々に共通の認識をこのモデルによって与えることができた。

この本が出版され、プロのテクニックを参考にデザイナーが自らモデルを創り自分のイメージやアイデアを表現できるようになればすばらしいことだと思う。

Making a model for each stage of planning is the best way that I have found to express the 3-D world that I have in my head so that a third party can understand it. Mr. Kurabayashi is that important person who makes the models by accurately reading my intentions from sometimes just a simple sketch or basic plan that I draw, or at other times from a detailed implementation plan. For more than 10 years he has also been my good friend.

The photos in this page are of model from a 21-hectare waterfront development master plan. These models have given and will give a great many people --the residents of the area, landowners and many who will become involved in the planning of the building--an idea of the overall image of this town that will be realized in the 21st century adjacent to the high-rise building.

With the publication of this book, it is my hope that designers will be able to use the techniques of the professional modeler as reference to express their own images and ideas.

Shunji Itoh
Itoh Space Institute

伊東俊二
伊東空間研究所代表

横浜市都市計画局開発部
ポートサイド開発事務所

*Yokohama City Planning Bureau,
Development Section,
Portside Development Office*

パーツ紹介
INTRODUCING VARIOUS PARTS

■ プラストラクトパターンシート PLASTRUCT PATTERNED SHEETS

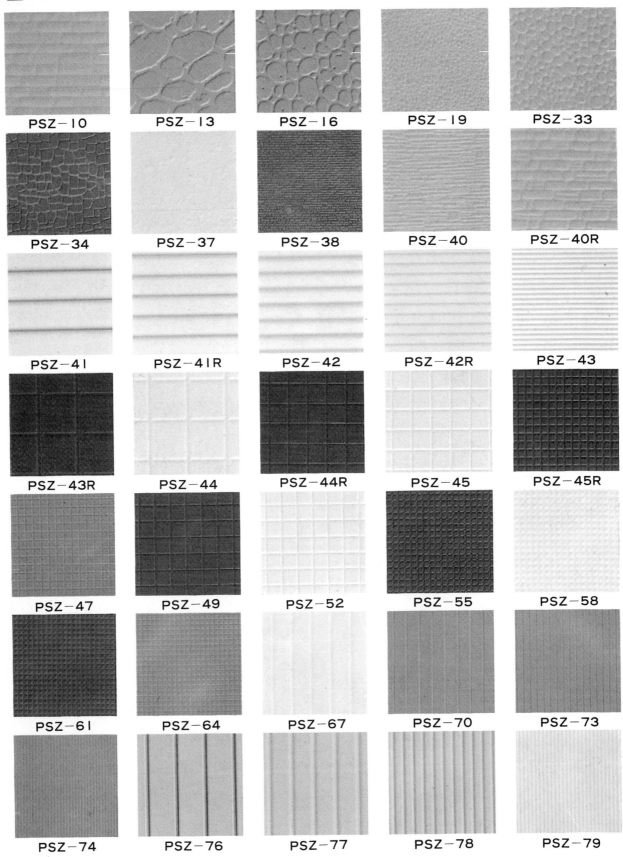

PSZ-10	PSZ-13	PSZ-16	PSZ-19	PSZ-33
PSZ-34	PSZ-37	PSZ-38	PSZ-40	PSZ-40R
PSZ-41	PSZ-41R	PSZ-42	PSZ-42R	PSZ-43
PSZ-43R	PSZ-44	PSZ-44R	PSZ-45	PSZ-45R
PSZ-47	PSZ-49	PSZ-52	PSZ-55	PSZ-58
PSZ-61	PSZ-64	PSZ-67	PSZ-70	PSZ-73
PSZ-74	PSZ-76	PSZ-77	PSZ-78	PSZ-79

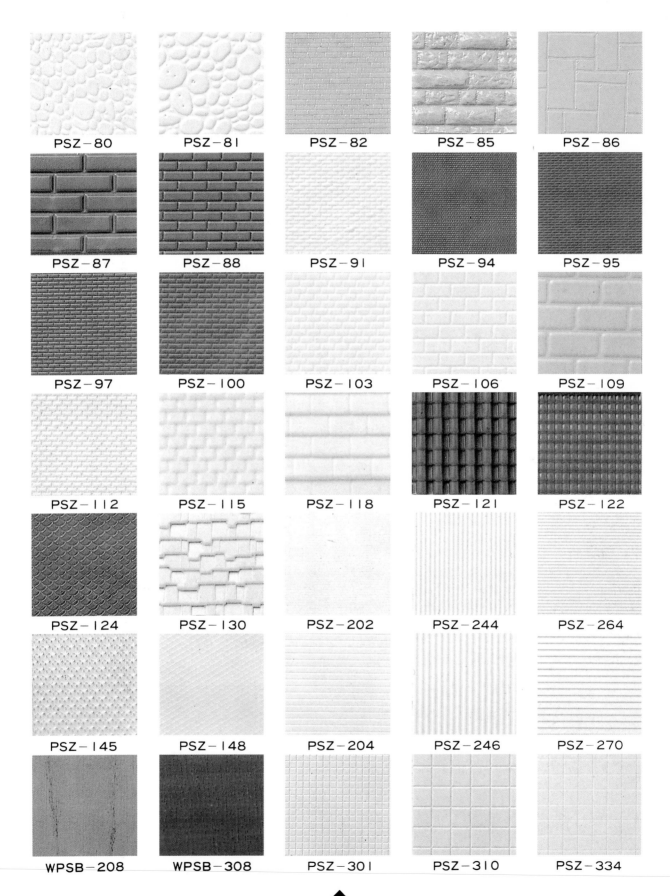

PSZ－80	PSZ－81	PSZ－82	PSZ－85	PSZ－86
PSZ－87	PSZ－88	PSZ－91	PSZ－94	PSZ－95
PSZ－97	PSZ－100	PSZ－103	PSZ－106	PSZ－109
PSZ－112	PSZ－115	PSZ－118	PSZ－121	PSZ－122
PSZ－124	PSZ－130	PSZ－202	PSZ－244	PSZ－264
PSZ－145	PSZ－148	PSZ－204	PSZ－246	PSZ－270
WPSB－208	WPSB－308	PSZ－301	PSZ－310	PSZ－334

■ソファー SOFAS

No.1 1/20

No.2 1/30 1/20

No.3 1/50 1/30 1/20

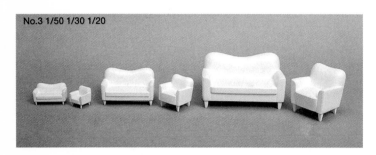

No.4 1/50 1/30 1/20

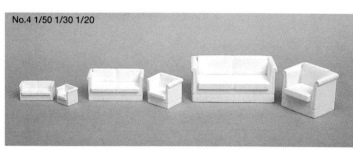

No.5 1/50

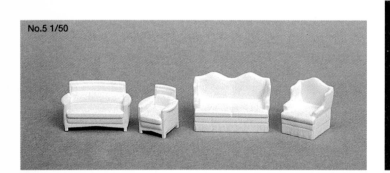

■椅子 CHAIRS

No.6 1/20 1/30 1/20 1/30

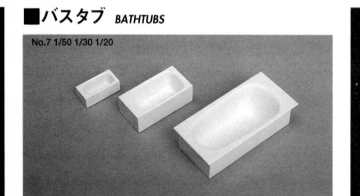

■バスタブ BATHTUBS

No.7 1/50 1/30 1/20

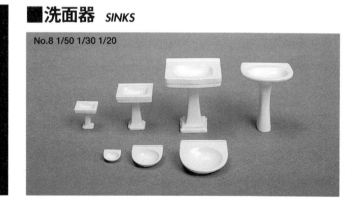

■洗面器 SINKS

No.8 1/50 1/30 1/20

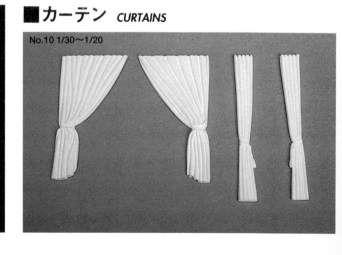

■便器 TOILETS

No.9 1/50 1/30 1/20

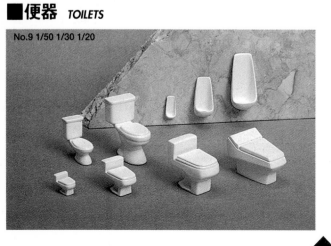

■カーテン CURTAINS

No.10 1/30～1/20

■プラスチック棒 PLASTIC RODS

コード	サイズ'D'mm	サイズ'W'mm
SAR—4	3.2	3.2
SAR—8	3.2	6.4
SAR—12	3.2	9.5

長さ380mm

ABS製・角棒 ABS ROD
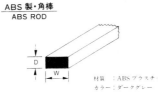

材質：ABSプラスチック
カラー：ダークグレー

コード	直径mm
AR—2	1.6
AR—4	3.2
AR—6	4.8
AR—8	6.4
AR—10	7.9
AR—12	9.5
AR—14	11.1
AR—16	12.7
AR—18	14.3
AR—20	15.9
AR—24	19.1
AR—28	22.2
AR—32	25.4
AR—36	28.6

長さ445mm

透明アクリル丸棒 CLEAR ACRYLIC ROUND ROD
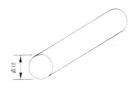

コード	サイズ'A'mm
ASR—4	3.2
ASR—8	6.4
ASR—12	9.5
ASR—16	12.7
ASR—20	15.9
ASR—24	19.1
ASR—32	25.4

長さ445mm

透明アクリル四角棒 CLEAR ACRYLIC SQUARE ROD
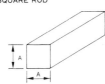

コード	サイズAmm	サイズBmm
ARR—5	3.2	15.9
ARR—7	4.8	19.1
ARR—8	6.4	12.7
ARR—9	6.4	25.4
ARR—23	19.1	25.4

長さ445mm

透明アクリル長四角棒 CLEAR ACRYLIC RECTANGULAR ROD

コード	サイズAmm
AHR—16	12.7
AHR—20	15.9
AHR—24	19.1
AHR—32	25.4

長さ445mm

透明アクリル半丸棒 CLEAR ACRYLIC HALF ROUND ROD
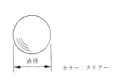

コード	サイズAmm
ATR—16	12.7
ATR—20	15.9
ATR—24	19.1
ATR—32	25.4

長さ445mm

透明アクリル三角棒 CLEAR ACRYLIC TRIANGULAR ROD
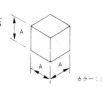

45°

コード	直径mm
AB—4	3.2
AB—6	4.8
AB—8	6.4
AB—12	9.5
AB—16	12.7
AB—20	15.9
AB—24	19.1
AB—28	22.2
AB—32	25.4
AB—40	31.8

アクリル球 ACRYLIC BALLS
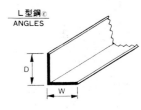

直径
カラー：クリアー

コード	サイズAmm
AC—8	6.4
AC—12	9.5
AC—16	12.7
AC—20	15.9
AC—24	19.1
AC—32	25.4
AC—40	31.8

アクリル角 ACRYLIC CUBES
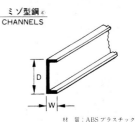

カラー：クリアー

■プラスチック製細角棒 STYRENE MICROSTRIP

正確にモールドされた断面が正方形と長方形の角棒です。
切断、折り曲げ、熱加工が簡単に出来ます。
表面が滑らかですので塗装も簡単です。
ABS・アクリルへの接着も可能です。
各種サイズが揃っております。精密模型にお使いください。

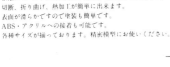

長さ330mm

コード	サイズA	サイズB
MSS—102	0.25	0.5
MSS—103	0.25	0.8
MSS—104	0.25	1.0
MSS—106	0.25	1.5
MSS—108	0.25	2.0
MSS—110	0.25	2.5
MSS—112	0.25	3.2
MSS—116	0.25	4.0
MSS—119	0.25	4.8
MSS—125	0.25	6.4
MSS—152	0.4	0.5
MSS—153	0.4	0.8
MSS—154	0.4	1.0
MSS—156	0.4	1.5
MSS—158	0.4	2.0
MSS—1510	0.4	2.5
MSS—1512	0.4	3.2
MSS—1516	0.4	4.0
MSS—1519	0.4	4.8
MSS—1525	0.4	6.4
MSS—202	0.5	0.5
MSS—203	0.5	0.8
MSS—204	0.5	1.0
MSS—206	0.5	1.5
MSS—208	0.5	2.0
MSS—210	0.5	2.5
MSS—212	0.5	3.2
MSS—216	0.5	4.0
MSS—219	0.5	4.8
MSS—225	0.5	6.4
MSS—303	0.8	0.8
MSS—304	0.8	1.0
MSS—306	0.8	1.5
MSS—308	0.8	2.0
MSS—310	0.8	2.5
MSS—312	0.8	3.2

コード	サイズA	サイズB
MSS—316	0.8	4.0
MSS—319	0.8	4.8
MSS—325	0.8	6.4
MSS—404	1.0	1.0
MSS—406	1.0	1.5
MSS—408	1.0	2.0
MSS—410	1.0	2.5
MSS—412	1.0	3.2
MSS—416	1.0	4.0
MSS—419	1.0	4.8
MSS—425	1.0	6.4
MSS—606	1.5	1.5
MSS—608	1.5	2.0
MSS—610	1.5	2.5
MSS—612	1.5	3.2
MSS—616	1.5	4.0
MSS—619	1.5	4.8
MSS—625	1.5	6.4
MSS—808	2.0	2.0
MSS—810	2.0	2.5
MSS—812	2.0	3.2
MSS—816	2.0	4.0
MSS—819	2.0	4.8
MSS—825	2.0	6.4
MSS—1010	2.5	2.5
MSS—1012	2.5	3.2
MSS—1016	2.5	4.0
MSS—1019	2.5	4.8
MSS—1025	2.5	6.4
MSS—1212	3.2	3.2
MSS—1216	3.2	4.0
MSS—1219	3.2	4.8
MSS—1225	3.2	6.4

1袋5本入

材質：スチレンプラスチック
カラー：オペークホワイト

■型鋼材 STRUCTURAL STEEL SHAPES

この部材を使用しますと架構・鉄骨構造などの表現が簡単に出来ます。
ASBプラスチックですので切断・接着・塗装も容易です。

コード	実寸D×Wmm	長さmm
AZ—1	1.2×1.2	254
AZ—2	1.6×1.6	254
PSA—3	2.4×2.4	380
PSA—4	3.2×3.2	380
PSA—6	4.8×4.8	610
PSA—8	6.4×6.4	610
PSA—10	7.9×7.9	610
PSA—12	9.5×9.5	610

L型鋼 ANGLES
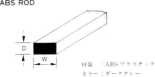

コード	実寸D×Wmm	長さmm
BZ—2	1.6×0.9	254
BZ—3	2.4×1.2	254
PSB—4	3.2×1.9	610

I型鋼 BEAMS

コード	実寸D×Wmm	長さmm
PSB—12	9.5×4.8	760
PSB—14	11.1×5.5	760
PSB—16	12.7×6.4	760
PSB—18	14.3×6.4	760
PSB—20	15.9×6.4	760
PSB—24	19.1×7.9	760
PSB—28	22.2×9.5	760
PSB—32	25.4×9.5	760
PSB—36	28.6×12.7	760

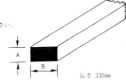

コード	実寸D×Wmm	長さmm
CZ—2	1.6×0.9	254
CZ—3	2.4×1.0	254
PSC—4	3.2×1.2	380
PSC—6	4.8×1.6	610
PSC—8	6.4×1.9	610
PSC—10	7.9×2.0	610
PSC—12	9.5×2.4	760
PSC—14	11.1×3.2	760
PSC—16	12.7×3.2	760
PSC—18	14.3×3.2	760
PSC—20	15.9×4.8	760
PSC—24	19.1×4.8	760

ミゾ型鋼 CHANNELS
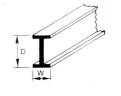

材質：ABSプラスチック
カラー：スチールグレー（SG）

'H' COLUMNS / H型鋼

コード	実寸D×Wmm	長さmm
HZ-2	1.6×1.6	254
HZ-3	2.4×2.4	380
PSH-4	3.2×3.2	610
PSH-6	4.8×4.8	610
PSH-8	6.4×6.4	760
PSH-10	7.9×7.9	760
PSH-12	9.5×9.5	760
PSH-14	11.1×11.1	760
PSH-16	12.7×12.7	760
PSH-18	14.3×14.3	760
PSH-20	15.9×15.9	760
PSH-24	19.1×19.1	760

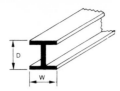

H型鋼 'H'COLUMNS

T型鋼ᴇ TEES

コード	実寸D×Wmm	長さmm
TZ-1	1.2×1.2	254
TZ-2	1.6×1.6	254
PST-3	2.4×2.4	380
PST-4	3.2×3.2	380
PST-6	4.8×4.8	610
PST-8	6.4×6.4	610

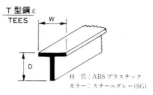

材　質：ABSプラスチック
カラー：スチールグレー(SG)

■コンクリート柱 *STRUCTURAL CONCRETE SHAPES*

長方形柱（管）RECTANGULAR TUBING

コード	実寸D×Wmm
FPB-8	6.4×4.8
FPB-10	7.9×6.4
FPB-12	9.5×6.4
FPB-14	11.1×6.4
FPB-16	12.7×6.4
FPB-18	14.3×6.4
FPB-19	14.3×9.5
FPB-20	15.9×6.4
FPB-21	15.9×12.7
FPB-24	19.1×95
FPB-26	19.1×143
FPB-28	22.2×9.5
FPB-29	22.2×15.9
FPB-32	25.4×9.5
FPB-33	25.4×19.1
FPB-36	28.6×95
FPB-37	28.6×19.1

材　質：ABSプラスチック
肉　厚：1.6mm
カラー：コンクリートグレー

長さはすべて760mmです

コード	実寸D×Wmm	長さmm
FPH-4	3.2×3.2	760
FPH-6	4.8×4.8	760
FPH-8	6.4×6.4	760
FPH-10	7.9×7.9	760
FPH-12	9.5×9.5	760
FPH-14	11.1×11.1	760
FPH-16	12.7×12.7	760
FPH-18	14.3×14.3	760
FPH-20	15.9×15.9	760
FPH-24	19.1×19.1	760
FPH-28	22.2×22.2	760
FPH-32	25.4×25.4	760
FPH-36	28.6×28.6	760
FPH-40	31.8×31.8	760

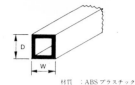

正方形柱（管）ᴇ SQUARE TUBING

材質　：ABSプラスチック
肉厚　：1.6mm
カラー：コンクリートグレー

コード	サイズA×B	適用コンクリート柱
CB-12	9.5×7.1	FPH-12
CB-14	9.5×7.9	FPH-14
CB-16	9.5×9.5	FPH-16
CB-18	12.7×11.1	FPH-18
CB-20	12.7×12.7	FPH-20
CB-24	15.9×15.9	FPH-24

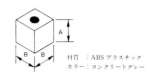

コンクリート柱用ブロックᴇ CONCRETE BLOCKS

材質　：ABSプラスチック
カラー：コンクリートグレー

コード	直径mm	長さmm
MR-10	0.25	254
MR-20	0.5	254
MR-25	0.6	356
MR-30	0.8	254
MR-35	0.9	356
MR-40	1.0	254
MR-45	1.1	356
MR-50	1.3	254
MR-60	1.5	356

1袋10本入

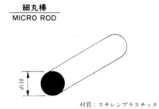

細丸棒 MICRO ROD

材質：スチレンプラスチック

スチレンプラスチック製の細い丸棒です。
今まで金属棒でしか表現出来なかったものにも利用出来ます。
切断、曲げ、接着が簡単に出来ます。

■パイプ *PIPES*

760mm ／ 900mm

コード	直径mm
P-( )-1	0.8
P-( )-2	1.6
P-( )-3	2.4
P-( )-4	3.2
P-( )-6	4.8
P-( )-8	6.4
P-( )-10	7.9
P-( )-12	9.5
P-( )-14	11.1
P-( )-16	12.7
P-( )-18	14.3
P-( )-20	15.9
P-( )-24	19.1
P-( )-28	22.2
P-( )-32	25.4
P-( )-36	28.6
P-( )-40	31.8

材質：ブチレイトプラスチック

コード	直径mm
VT-150	38.1
VT-175	44.5
VT-200	50.8
VT-225	57
VT-250	63
VT-275	70
VT-300	76
VT-325	82
VT-350	88
VT-375	95
VT-400	102
VT-425	108
VT-450	114
VT-475	120
VT-500	127
VT-525	133
VT-550	140
VT-575	146
VT-600	152

材質：ABS
肉厚：VT-150～300　2.4mm
　　　VT-325～600　3.2mm

ⓔ　P-1, P-2はプラスチック被覆線です。
　　P-3, P-4には中に真鍮ロッドを入れ曲げて
　　使用することが出来ます。
　　カラーは各色そろっております。
　　P-1～VT-200までは次の様な色があります。

大きさ	R	Y	B	G	O	W	BK	BR	VL	VG	P	EG	T	LB
1-4	○	○	○	○	○	○	○	○	○	○	○	○	○	○
6-8	○	○	○	○	○	○	○	○	○	○	○	○	○	
10-40	○	○	○	○	○	○	○	○	○	○	○	○		
150-200	○	○	○	○	○	○	○				○			

R-赤、Y-黄、B-青、G-緑、O-オレンジ、
W-白、BK-黒、BR-ブラウン、VL-バイ
オレット、VG-パルプグレー、P-ピンク、
EG-エレクトリカルグリーン、T-タン、LB-ライトブルー

ご注文の場合はP-R-2の様に（　）の中に色のコードを入れてください。
配管用に使用の場合は、エンジニアリングモデル用パーツカタログをご覧ください。

真鍮棒ᴇ BRASS RODS

コード	適用パイプ
BRO-47	P-3
BRO-60	P-4

長さ：760mm

■フェンス *FENCING*

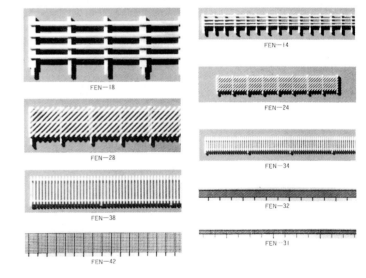

FEN-18
FEN-28
FEN-38
FEN-42
FEN-14
FEN-24
FEN-34
FEN-32
FEN-31

コード	適用縮尺	種　類	全　長(mm)
FEN-14	1/100	4本横木	510
FEN-18	1/50	4本横木	760
FEN-24	1/100	斜め木さく	510
FEN-28	1/50	斜め木さく	760
FEN-31	1/500	立て木さく	1900
FEN-32	1/200	立て木さく	1300
FEN-34	1/100	立て木さく	510
FEN-38	1/50	立て木さく	760
FEN-42	1/200	チェーンリンク	660

品物はそれぞれ適当に分割されて袋に入っています。
全長はトータル寸法です。
FEN-31, 32, 42を除いて材質は白のスチレンプラスチックです。
FEN-31, 32, 42は0.2mm真鍮板のエッチングです。

■人形 *FIGURES*

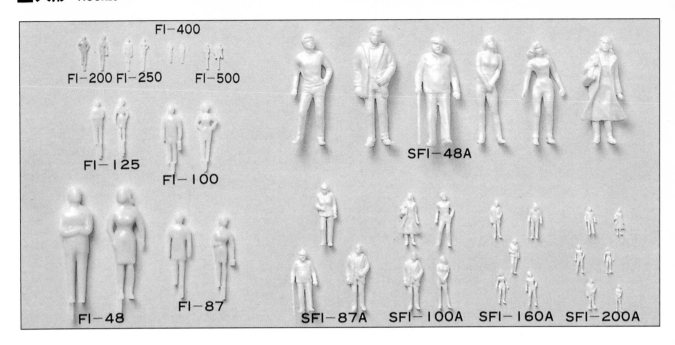

FI-400

FI-200 FI-250 FI-500

FI-125

FI-100

SFI-48A

FI-48

FI-87

SFI-87A SFI-100A SFI-160A SFI-200A

■自動車 *PLASTIC VEHICLES*

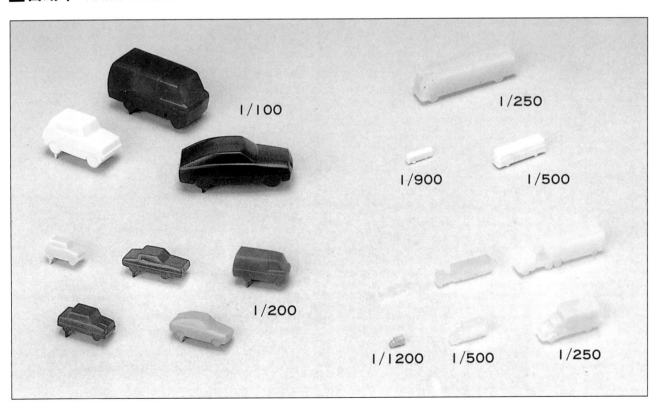

1/100

1/250

1/900

1/500

1/200

1/1200

1/500

1/250

■階段 *CUSTOM STAIRCASES/STEPS/STAIRS*

階段A
CUSTOM STAIRCASES

コード	適用縮尺	タイプ	踏枚の段数
STAA—24	1/25	直 進 階 段	14
STAA—48	1/50	直 進 階 段	14
STAL—24	1/25	左曲り急折階段	4
STAL—48	1/50	左曲り急折階段	5
STAR—24	1/25	右曲り急折階段	4
STAR—48	1/50	右曲り急折階段	5
STAS—24	1/25	ら せ ん 階 段	14
STAS—48	1/50	ら せ ん 階 段	14

材質 ：スチレンプラスチック
組立式

直進階段 　　　　　らせん階段

右曲り急折階段 　　　　　左曲り急折階段

直進階段と急折階段は組み合わせて一緒に使えます。

階段B
STEPS

コード	適用縮尺	スタイル	実寸W×L mm
STEP—1	1/400	B	50.8×25.4
STEP—2	1/200	B	73×34.9
STEP—4	1/100	B	73×34.9
STEP—8	1/50	A	178×305
STEP—12	1/30	A	178×305

スタイルAはスチンシートの成形品です。
スタイルBはスチレンのインジェクションモールドです。

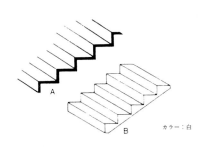

カラー：白

階段C ⒠
STAIRS

コード	適用縮尺	相当巾 mm	踏板の実寸巾 mm	実寸巾 mm
ST—4	1/100	950	7.9	9.5
ST—6	1/50	955	15.9	19.1
ST—8		1110	19.1	22.2
ST—12	1/30	858	23.8	28.6
ST—14		1000	28.6	33.3
ST—16	1/25	913	31.8	365
ST—18		1070	38.1	42.8
ST—20	1/15	786	47.6	52.4
ST—22		940	57.2	62.7

長さ　ST—4　127mm
　　　ST6～22　300mm
材質　：ABS
カラー：スチールグレー

---

p.136から紹介されている商品は、模型を製作する上で必要なパーツの
一部です。詳しい案内書、パンフレット、ご注文をご希望の方は下記の
住所までお問い合わせ下さい。

㈱アトリエエスキース
〒142 東京都品川区西中延1-3-7 扶桑ハイツ301
Tel.03（3788）0671　Fax.03（3784）3539

あとがきに
かえて

POSTSCRIPT

　早いもので月刊「室内」で模型の作り方を1年間にわたり掲載してからすでに6年になります。その後、産業調査会から出版された「インテリア」の中に模型の作り方を掲載しました。そしてここに4年の月日をかけてようやく本書を出版することになりました。この企画を進めていく上で最大の苦労といえば、なんといっても毎回の撮影でした。5000カットにもおよぶ撮影を終えると同時に写真の選択、それに添付するキャプションの執筆と苦労の連続でした。

　「もうこんな作業は二度とゴメンだ」と思う反面「ああすればよかった」「こうすればよかった」「もっと分かりやすい文章は」などと後悔はつきません。もう「これで完璧」ということがないのが模型作りの世界なのでしょう。

　とりあえずはここで終わりにしようと思います。これからの企画として店舗模型、住宅模型、ビル模型、地形模型の作り方などを図面から完成のプロセスを一冊の中にまとめる予定です。皆さんのご意見やご感想がありましたらお聞かせください。これからの企画の参考にさせていただきます。

　本書を出版するにあたり協力していただいた方、またそのきっかけとなった「室内」の皆さん、そして「産業調査会」の皆さん、この場を借りてお礼を申し上げます。そして読者の皆さんの作品製作に少しでもこの本が役立つことを心から願いつつペンをおきたいと思います。ありがとうございました。

Six years have rushed by since my model-making processes were serialized in the monthly magazine "Shitsunai" (Interiors). These processes have since been published in "Interior" magazine put out by the Industrial Research Center of Japan Inc. Production Goods Workstation. It has taken four full years to finally complete this book. The most difficult part was taking the photos of each step. Over 5,000 shots were taken, and the proper photos had to be selected and the descriptions written.

Sometimes it has been so much trouble that I swore I would never make a book like this again, but now I feel glad that I have. Also sometimes I think, "if I had just done it this way or written a simpler description like this..." There is no end to such thoughts. I cannot say I am fully satisfied, but I suppose that is inherent in the world of model-making.

Anyway, the book is now in your hands. The next project I am planning is to put into one book the entire model-making process from drawing to completion for several models, including store models, house models, building models and landscape models. Please feel free to contact me with your ideas and impressions. I will take them into consideration for upcoming projects.

I would like to take this opportunity to thank everyone who helped to make this book possible, everyone at "Shitsunai" to whom I owe the idea for this book, and everyone at the Industrial Research Center of Japan Inc. Production Goods Workstation. Lastly I would like to say that I hope this can be of use to you, the reader, in making better interior models. Thank you.

著者略歴

1957年群馬県前橋市生まれ。1978年環境造形学園専門学校インテリアスクール、インテリアデザイン研究科修了後、住宅設計会社、店舗会社、施工会社を経て1981年創作工房アトリエエスキース創業。1982年株式会社アトリエエスキース設立。1989年インテリアセンタースクール講師、1993年付設学科プレゼンテーションテクニック科モデリングコース主任、現在に至る。

About the Author

Born in 1957 in Gunma Prefecture, Japan, the author completed training in the interior design and research departments of the vocational Interior Center School in 1978, was employed by residential design, store and construction firms until 1981 when he founded Atelier Esquisse, a design studio. In 1982 he established Atelier Esquisse Co. Ltd. In 1989 the author was hired to teach modeling at the Interior Center School.

インテリア模型製作

1994年10月25日　初版第 1 刷発行

著　者―――倉林　進 ©

発行者―――久世利郎

印　刷―――凸版印刷(新嘉坡)私人有限公司

発行所―――株式会社グラフィック社

　　　　〒102 東京都千代田区九段北1-9-12

　　　　Tel.03(3263)4318　Fax.03(3263)5297

　　　　振替　00130-6-114345

　　　　ISBN4-7661-0798-5 C3052